MAKERS OF
CHRISTIANITY

MAKERS OF
CHRISTIANITY

FROM JESUS TO CHARLEMAGNE

BY

SHIRLEY JACKSON CASE

KENNIKAT PRESS
Port Washington, N. Y./London

MAKERS OF CHRISTIANITY

Copyright 1934 by Holt, Rinehart and Winston, Inc.
Copyright (c) 1962 by Shirley Jackson Case
Reissued in 1971 by Kennikat Press by arrangement
with Holt, Rinehart and Winston, Inc.
Library of Congress Catalog Card No: 79-118460
ISBN 0-8046-1402-4

Manufactured by Taylor Publishing Company   Dallas, Texas

ESSAY AND GENERAL LITERATURE INDEX REPRINT SERIES

CONTENTS

PREFACE

This book sketches the first eight centuries of Christianity's history—an old story told in a new way. The Christian movement is presented in terms of the living people who constituted its membership and who were especially prominent in giving it direction and continuity. Thus history is depicted as a process of life.

Visiting cemeteries to decipher old tombstones may satisfy a morbid curiosity, but excursions among the dead are a poor substitute for personal companionship with the living. Historical study has too often been a sepulchral discipline. It has consisted in gleaning dates and proper names from ancient documents treated as if they were cemetery inscriptions. In the present volume an effort has been made to walk with the people of the past upon their own highways, to feel the realities they felt in life, and to participate sympathetically in the tasks that engaged their attention. It is this emphasis that gives to the present volume its distinctiveness.

The needs of the layman have been kept definitely in mind. He may read as he runs. There are no footnotes to halt his progress or deflect his interest. But this book may also be used as a textbook for class study. The appended "Selected Bibliography" furnishes suggestions for further reading on the subject matter of each chapter. A course of study adapted to the needs of various groups may easily be set up by grading the supplementary reading according to the needs of the students. The story of Christianity's past, whether studied in church schools, colleges, or seminaries, will become much more attractive when approached from the biographical point of view.

S. J. C.

The Divinity School
The University of Chicago
July 27, 1934

INTRODUCTION

Man is a great builder; he has been a maker of many things. At the very dawn of history he appeared in this aggressive rôle. He devised crude instruments to aid him in his quest for food and shelter. By whirling a wooden drill, or striking sparks from hard flint, he invented fire to cook his food and warm his habitation. Applying his constructive skill in the arts of agriculture and navigation, he slowly subjected both land and sea to his will. In the long course of the centuries he has built roads, invented engines, bridged rivers, tunneled mountains, conquered the air, organized vast industries, accumulated fabulous wealth, and bound continent to continent with telegraph cables, radio communication, and globe-encircling routes of commerce. Slowly but surely he has mastered mightily his physical environment.

Man is also a builder of culture. The invention of language, together with the art of writing and printing, has made possible the preservation of knowledge accumulating from generation to generation and its dissemination over the face of the earth. Civilization's advance has waited upon the emergence in society of poets, musicians, painters, sculptors, architects, philosophers, scientists, educators, statesmen, who have proved themselves capable of keen feeling, clear thinking and vigorous action. Without these triumphs of the human mind in the realm of aesthetic, moral and spiritual values, past ages would be a dreary stretch of time. The work of men has been necessary to make this desert blossom as the rose.

In all cultural history, religion has always occupied a conspicuous place. Herein, again, man has been a great builder. In his efforts to bring the mysterious forces of the universe into the service of needy mortals he has devised elaborate rituals, fashioned innumerable creeds and established formidable religious institutions. Among all the peoples of the earth—Egyptians, Babylonians, Persians, Hindus, Chinese, Japanese, Greeks, Romans, Jews, Arabs, Africans, Europeans, Americans—from the most primitive types of civilization to the most highly developed, men have busied themselves extensively with religious activities. Diviners, priests, prophets, legislators, preachers, teachers, reformers, and a host of lesser ministrants, have dedicated their energies to the establishment and perpetuation of one or another religion.

Among the ancient religions of mankind, that of the Hebrews was unique in the prominence it gave to creative leaders. The patriarch, Abraham, was the heroic figure through whom his descendants had obtained the blessings of an everlasting covenant with God. Moses was the revered leader who had been entrusted with the task of communicating the divine law to the chosen people. Judges and kings were God's representatives appointed to administer the affairs of government. Great prophets were men through whom the Deity called upon sinners to repent if they would escape impending judgment. Priests were the divinely appointed performers of the temple ritual and the guardians of the holy vessels. Scribes and rabbis, educated in sacred lore, were the authentic teachers of the people. In every phase of religion's operations consecrated men were essential to its effective maintenance. A pious Psalmist could fittingly declare that man was well-nigh the equal of God, who had crowned him with glory and honor. The history of the ancient Hebrew and Jewish religion is essentially the life-story of the human agents whom God was believed to have employed in its making and re-making through the course of the centuries.

Christianity inherited from Judaism a high regard for the human agent in the operations of religion. Early missionaries passed this ideal along to their Gentile converts, who were admonished to work out their own salvation with fear and trembling under the conviction that God was working in and through them toward the accomplishment of his purposes. Worthy religion demanded capable persons for its making. How well, or how poorly, these makers of Christianity discharged their task is revealed in the history of the religion's growth as the story of its past is read in terms of the activities of those more aggressive and industrious individuals whom the church drew into its service.

Preachers fired with prophetic zeal launched the new religious movement in Palestine nineteen hundred years ago. They were followed by missionary evangelists who carried their gospel to the principal centers of population around the Mediterranean world then unified under the rule of Roman emperors. As the congregations multiplied, adding to their membership persons of different heritages and tastes, the leaders of the growing enterprise presently awakened to the need for a more efficient organization and government of the Christian societies. Until a standardized institutional machinery had been created, divergent tendencies within the several churches increasingly threatened the perpetuity and integrity of Christendom. Eminent in the history of early Christianity are those persons who during the second and third centuries diligently devoted themselves to building up a substantial ecclesiastical institution.

Various skills and equipments were needed for the tasks that fell to the hand of Christianity's leaders. Within its cultural environment the new religion had a host of rivals and not a few bitter enemies. Happily for its success, it attracted to its ranks some converts who had been schooled in different phases of the contemporary civilization and who were thus equipped to become successful champions of the Christian cause. Not only did their presence contribute significantly to the cultural respectability of the new enterprise, but their ability to use the current weapons of apologetic warfare rendered invaluable service to Christianity in its conflict with rival religions and philosophies, as well as with its political foes. Thanks to the devoted service of these leaders, Christianity's social triumph was ultimately accomplished and the once despised cult became in time the only legal religion for the entire Roman world.

The makers of Christianity were compelled to face many new tasks as the political structure of the empire ruled by Augustus and his successors began to crumble. In the East, where the imperial régime still maintained itself intact for several centuries, the demand for aggressive and creative Christian leadership was somewhat dulled by the undisturbed continuance of the established social order, at least until the rise of the Mohammedan power in the seventh century. But in the West a very different set of circumstances confronted the church. Invaders from the north swarmed into Italy, Gaul, Spain, and North Africa early in the fifth century. Barbarian rulers established separate kingdoms in the territories that had formerly been unified under Roman sway. The social foundations on which an imperial state church had been reared in the West were violently shaken. Serious problems now challenged Christianity; its leaders were forced to pioneer on new frontiers. Creative Christian leadership was not wanting in the new crisis. The church, now the most stable institution in Western society, had to assume many new responsibilities. Bishops, who had formerly been free to devote themselves exclusively to ecclesiastical affairs, and who had been relieved of civic or municipal obligations by the favoring legislation of Christian emperors, had now to take on such secular tasks as supervising repairs on the aqueducts, distributing the corn doles, conducting political negotiations, or discharging other unecclesiastical duties, in order to preserve a modicum of social well-being amid the disturbed conditions of the times. Christian leaders, when competent for the work and sensitive to the demands of the hour, served both church and state. Thus Christianity assumed guardianship over the total range of society's concerns. A forceful Christian bishop, like Gregory the Great, was a veritable statesman; while a zealous Christian monarch, like Charlemagne, was as much a maker of Christianity as he was a restorer of the western Roman Empire.

In attempting to review the history of ancient Christianity by employing the biographical approach, one will do well to note that the makers of the Christian movement lived and worked in close touch with their fellow-men. They shared their companions' experiences, thought their thoughts, participated in their activities, and personified their hopes. Biographical history, to be genuinely illuminating, must view conspicuous persons as facets, mirrors, types, of the age and society to which they belonged.

Outstanding historical individuals were, however, not simply passive channels through which the common life of the past flowed with concentrated power into the present. They were also creators, whose initiative, originality and aggressiveness gave momentum to the stream and kept society's expanding life from growing stagnant. They were the agitating spirits that troubled the face of the waters.

Mere mass humanity seems unable, of itself, to rise to the highest possibilities of existence; until capable leaders emerge progress lags. While effective leaders are always men of their own day, sharing abundantly in the life of their fellows, they exhibit also in some unusual degree ability to effect the release of fresh ideas or ideals, a power to concentrate upon some slumbering interest, a self-sacrificing readiness to serve some worthy cause, a new insight into life's values, a peculiar capacity for organizing hitherto incoherent yearnings, or an inspiring personal devotion to a timely enterprise. One or more of these characteristics makes them conspicuous. They are the creative individuals who, in religion as in any other sphere, keep mankind moving forward to the better things that are yet to be.

CHAPTER I

HERALDS OF A NEW DAY

The prophet hates hypocrisy; he is the implacable enemy of all shams. The vainglory of outward show is offensive to his simple tastes, ceremonious respectability passes for naught with him, complacent formalism arouses his disgust. His gaze penetrates beneath the surface of appearances to the motives that actuate men's conduct. Insincerity, duplicity, selfishness, he cannot tolerate. Deeds, not words, are the measure of one's real worth. The tree is to be judged, not by the gaudy colors of its foliage and blossoms, but by the quality of its fruit.

It was in this prophetic temper that John the Baptist addressed his audiences in the Judean desert some nineteen hundred years ago. Like his predecessors in ancient Israel, he uttered burning words of condemnation and warning. His message was encumbered with none of the excuses or palliatives that a more considerate critic might have felt obliged to note. Oblivious of all else, he sought out what seemed to him the fundamental weakness of his contemporaries, against whose perversity his indignation blazed forth with the intensity of a powerful searchlight. His words were like arrows dipped in fire and brimstone: You sons of treachery, do you think you have learned how to escape the fury of the judgment day? Absurd! Show the genuineness of your repentance by your conduct. You trust in your descent from Abraham—an empty formality in the sight of

1

God. The time of reckoning is at hand, when the Almighty will purge his holy land in readiness for the dawn of a new day.

This stormy prophet, John, was an impressive figure. Coarsely garbed, and subsisting on the simple food obtainable in his desert environment, he personified the repudiation of these cultural vanities condemned in his preaching. He was the type of reformer who by example and precept would liberate the individual from bondage to the artificialities of an effete social order. Trust in worldly possessions, attachment to traditional institutions, and other habitual quests or activities that had become the chief aim of life, were declared to be of quite secondary importance and capable of absolute renunciation. John was an exponent of a form of Jewish idealism that pictured the early destruction of the present world by a sudden act of God, and the pious prophet repudiated beforehand those ways of living that were about to be abolished by divine intervention.

Some of John's hearers were so favorably impressed with the man and his preaching that they joined his religious movement by accepting the rite of baptism at his hands. Thus they pledged themselves to the new ideals of righteousness proclaimed in his sermons and thereby they sought release from the baneful consequences of former contact with the sinful world. They still lived therein, but at longer range from its entanglements and with a new determination to frown upon its wickedness. Refusing to be distracted by the transient externalities of their present existence, they reconsecrated themselves to the divine will and were confident that God would presently deliver them from their distresses. This new program for specialization in righteousness was John's distinctive contribution toward the remaking of the Jewish religion of his day.

JESUS

Jesus, a carpenter from Nazareth, was among those who went down to the Jordan valley to hear John's enkindling call to repentance in preparation for God's new order. This cause appealed to Jesus with compelling power. He abandoned his workshop in Nazareth, even mother and brothers and sisters being left henceforth to shift for themselves, and, convinced that God had summoned him to a new task, he embarked upon the career of a prophetic religious reformer. But, unlike John, he forsook the fastness of the desert and sought out men on the common highways of life. As occasion offered he preached in country, village and city, delivering his message to fellow travelers, to congregations in the synagogues, or to groups informally assembled in the open country or on the city streets.

Jesus lived in trying times. Palestine had fallen into the hands of the Romans in 63 B.C. Henceforth the yoke of the foreigner had grown constantly heavier, while his desecrations of the Holy Land multiplied. Although Rome had permitted Herod the Great to rule as king of the Jews (37-4 B.C.), his professed loyalty to the Jewish religion had not checked the rising tide of heathen defilements in God's sacred territory. Taxes collected from the people were freely expended for building temples in honor of Emperor Augustus even within Palestine itself, and characteristic Roman entertainments were staged almost under the shadow of the Jewish temple at Jerusalem. In the two chief cities of Palestine, Jerusalem in Judea and Sepphoris in Galilee, foreigners, with their wares and customs, were almost as much at home as were Jews. People in authority, who enjoyed the king's favor, might approve of his cosmopolitanism, but the devout Jew, yielding allegiance only to God as his king and ruler, viewed the situation with disgust and righteous indignation.

Herod's death in 4 B.C. was the signal for outraged Jews to act. A certain Judas, heading a band of Galilean revolutionaries, seized weapons from the royal armory in the capital, Sepphoris, and attempted to establish once more Jewish autonomy under the protection of God. But presently the people of Sepphoris were to pay dearly for their ambition. Roman soldiers, aided by the army of King Aretas of Arabia, destroyed the city, slaughtering or carrying into captivity its inhabitants. During the next quarter-century under the patronage of Herod Antipas, to whom the Romans assigned control of Galilee (4 B.C.-39 A.D.), Sepphoris was magnificently rebuilt. It continued to be the royal residence until Tiberias was founded (about 25 A.D.), and it still blended in its life as a Jewish city those foreign elements that defiled the purity of God's chosen land and people.

While this tempestuous chapter in Jewish history was taking form Jesus was growing to manhood in the neighboring village of Nazareth, scarcely an hour's walk from Sepphoris. Here he had observed at close range, during the impressionable period of youth and early maturity, concrete events illustrative of a wide area of Jewish experience in these stirring times. Gladly would one hear more about Jesus' feelings and activities during this obscure period in his career. Had some of his own kindred been slain or taken captive when the Romans avenged themselves on the once rebellious city of Sepphoris? Had he plied his trade there as a laborer during the years of the city's rebuilding? Had he meditated upon the future of God's people mingling with foreigners amid the complexities of an urban environment? Remembering Sepphoris' fate, had he learned for all time to come the futility of attempting, either by the violence of open revolt advocated by his zealous compatriots, or by withdrawal into the seclusion of the desert after the manner of a John the Baptist, to establish the Kingdom of God in Palestine?

These questions may easily be asked, but in the present state of our information they cannot be decisively answered. Yet the background out of which they arise ought not to be ignored. This was the realistic setting from which Jesus came when he joined the company that assembled to hear John's flaming summons to repentance in preparation for the approaching Day of Judgment. And Jesus returned to a similar complexity of social conditions in Capernaum, and other centers of Jewish life, when he entered upon his own aggressive activity as a herald of the new day that he envisaged for his kinsmen.

The religiously sensitive individual, who remained in intimate association with common folk in Palestine, had ample opportunity to become keenly aware of the distressing situation under which the Jewish people were then living. They cherished memories of a day in the remote past when God had covenanted with their ancestors to bestow upon them his perpetual favor and make Palestine their sanctified dwelling place. But this ideal still remained an unfulfilled hope. In the early decades of the present era the actual status of the Palestinian Jew under Roman domination contrasted sharply with their cherished vision of a pure theocracy, in which God's will would be everywhere regnant and all evils would disappear from human society.

The Kingdom of God and the Kingdom of the Romans were incompatibles; the one could prevail only as the other perished. But Jewish piety could never concede the possibility of God's defeat, however long the manifestation of his triumph might be delayed. It was the distinctive task of religion to help man retain his trust in God and obey faithfully the divine will even in the darkest hour of national calamity. The crisis furnished the potential leader his golden opportunity. If he were equal to the occasion, he presented some original interpretation of current events, he advocated a line of conduct with specific reference to the immediate situation, and he reinforced confidence in the ultimate victory of good over evil.

The effective religious reformer is always a man of his own age. Its peculiar problems are his chief concern and heritages from its past furnish the materials with which he works. To establish a new religious sect is not his primary ambition. When stubborn resistance from his environment forces him and his followers into isolation, compelling the formation of a rival group, he may accept with a measure of equanimity this inevitable outcome. But it represents a lesser attainment than that toward which he had originally aspired. He would have preferred to rehabilitate ancient ideals, to restore the purity of earlier days, to reform a degenerate present, and to give healthful direction to the moral and spiritual energies of his contemporaries, all with a view to realizing privileges that were a rightful possession of descendants from noble ancestors. The prophetic reformer within Judaism always visualized the future Kingdom of God as the proper inheritance of the Jewish race.

The task undertaken by Jesus was made especially difficult by the existence of a well-fixed body of current opinion
as to what procedure would prove most effective in bringing about a fresh display of divine favor for the afflicted
people. The operations of Jewish religion were already
highly organized. Since ancient institutions had acquired
vested rights, loyalty to the established machinery of the
cult was readily assumed to insure the fullest possible measure of God's approval for the worshiper. The psychology
of institutionalism is of necessity hostile to changes in religion, as in all other areas of social activity. Techniques
and standards created to conserve past values ever tend to
become ends in themselves and thus obstruct the pathway
of an aggressive leader who fails to identify loyalty to party
or church with fidelity to his chosen cause. Jesus, like
many a Christian leader in later times, encountered relent-
less opposition from institutional authorities who so feared
the menace of innovations that they were unable to appreciate the prophet's zeal and vision.

Jesus' debt to Judaism, like Luther's heritage from
Roman Catholicism or John Wesley's obligation to the
Anglican Church, has not always been appraised at its full
value in later times. The needs of a new religious movement are thought to be best served by emphasizing the
originality of its idealized founder and minimizing his
agreements with his contemporaries. Certainly in the case
of Jesus reverence for the temple with its elaborate ritual
and the observance of the great festivals of the Jewish year
were vital factors in his religion. His debt to the devo-
tional and educational activities of the synagogue and the
rabbis and his allegiance to the Scriptures as the revelation
of God's will for his people were fundamental items in the

formation of Jesus' outlook and ideals. When he preached repentance and reconsecration, his message did not demand the repudiation of these religious heritages as a condition of securing God's greater favor. Not the institutions themselves, but the perfunctory or perverse manner in which he thought they were being perpetuated and interpreted by their present guardians, awakened his distrust or elicited his criticism.

Jesus did not aim primarily to displace the religious rites, customs or dogmas of Judaism. Rather, he sought to reform the people who were the heirs of this splendid inheritance. The past was not to be repudiated, but was to be worthily cherished, healthfully perpetuated and properly extended upon a higher level of efficiency. Slavish devotion to institutions needed to be redeemed by the cultivation of a new spiritual vitality, a further specialization in righteousness, motivated from within and fashioned in accordance with a standard of perfection exemplified by God himself. A renewed manifestation of divine favor for the chosen people awaited and demanded a new course of human action. Pursuing this path, Jesus would gladly have become, like the prophets of old, a new creative force in the remaking of Hebrew religion. But this was not to be the ultimate outcome of his labors.

When Jesus assumed the rôle of a religious reformer among his Palestinian contemporaries he ventured upon a precarious undertaking. The age was one of great confusion. There was a widespread conviction that the times were evil and that only by an unusual display of divine help could the sad state of affairs be rectified. But there was much diversity of effort and thinking with reference to the procedure by which the unfortunate situation might be corrected.

The Sadducean and priestly aristocracy was generally content to come to terms as best it could with the foreign rulers in order to secure from them by political negotiations a measure of local autonomy without sacrificing the emoluments and economic advantages to be derived from friendship with Rome. The Jewish people were now dispersed widely about the Mediterranean lands, especially in the larger cities like Antioch, Alexandria and Rome. From these thriving centers millions of Jews sent their annual assessment of two drachmæ, aggregating a vast sum, to the Jerusalem temple for the support of its priests and ceremonies. Emperors sometimes cast a covetous eye upon these Jewish levies, but the payments were not formally prohibited until the second century A.D. In view of this income the Jewish authorities at Jerusalem could well afford to concede the right of a Cæsar to collect from Palestinian Jews a yearly tax for the support of his government and could so far compromise with the heathen overlord as to offer daily sacrifice in his honor on the altar of Jehovah.

Many Palestinian Jews were far more provincially minded. They frowned upon the policies of their aristocratic leaders, resented the payment of tribute to Cæsar and deplored the invasion of their territory by heathen defilements. Yet not all devout Jews were of one opinion as to the proper remedial measures demanded by the situation. God was their common hope, but how their loyalty to his will should be displayed, or what manner of special service he required of them as preliminary to the divine deliverance, were questions variously answered by different persons and groups. Like men in modern times of distress who visualize in common the possibility of a more ideal social order, but differ as to the promise of success offered by a capitalist, fascist or communist program of action, the Jews of Palestine nineteen centuries ago were buffeted by conflicting opinions.

Standing out in sharp distinction from the aristocratic politicians, was the party popularly known as the Pharisees. Their characteristic emphasis was devotion to the sacred writings expounded by the learned rabbis and the regulation of life in accordance with the strict injunctions of the divine Law (Torah) by which God in times of old had revealed his holy will to his chosen people. While the Pharisees were loyal to the temple, their religious life drew its nourishment and inspiration more immediately from the activities of the synagogue. Through its ministrations they learned the divine will, receiving from properly equipped teachers the authentic interpretation of Scriptures regulative for the minutest details of living. To many Pharisees it must have seemed that the synagogue, with its attendant rabbis and their elaborate expositions of ancestral tradition, was the divinest of institutions. Learning in and obedience to the Law were readily assumed to insure a successful future for Israel. All else could be left to the inscrutable purposes of the Almighty.

The less well-schooled artisans and peasants, whose devotion to the Law was quite sincere but whose busy life afforded them slight opportunity for educational refinements, were often more impatient. Some of them were zealous for revolution. They eagerly attached themselves to Judas of Galilee, or any other prospective leader who gave promise of immediate action against the Romans. Since victory was to be given by God, neither the lack of an adventurer's military skill, nor his inadequate equipment and following, presented any serious obstacle to the popular imagination. All that was essential was a conviction that the favor of Heaven had at last been made manifest in the emergence and person of him who summoned his hearers to the unequal conflict. The atmosphere of Palestine was electric with revolutionary yearnings throughout the first century of the present era. The storm finally broke in full force in the year 66. When it had passed, the Jewish temple lay in ruins and even the semblance of national autonomy was completely shattered.

The preaching activity of Jesus fell, roughly speaking, at a point halfway between the death of Herod the Great in 4 B.C. and the destruction of the temple at Jerusalem by the Roman army under Titus in 70 A.D. It was a favorable moment for the advocate of a new cause to get a hearing. The public ear was wide open to any message of hope for relief from society's mounting ills. But the moment was equally perilous. Emotions ran high and nerves were on edge. The crowd was fickle, not from lack of seriousness but from desperation and uncertainty. Enthusiasms were likely to be volatile; loyalties might evaporate overnight. Religious and political authorities were wont to act on impulse under high tension, while the loud voice of expediency often drowned out the whispering protests of more sober judgment.

These circumstances held out to Jesus no glowing prospects of phenomenal success in his efforts to reform his compatriots in preparation for the advent of God's kingdom. Rival panaceas were too distractingly numerous and conflicting interests were too powerful to yield right of way to the socially obscure Nazarene preacher. He might well have hesitated to enter upon so precarious a venture, or have proceeded with cautious step carefully anticipating difficulties or deliberately weighing chances and probabilities. But the ardent prophet is not much given to prudential considerations. He forges ahead to his envisaged goal in straightforward pursuit of duty regardless of probable success or failure. His cause is God's cause, and therefore it cannot fail, whatever may overtake the prophet himself. So it was with Jesus. He made friends, when friends were available, and he boldly withstood his most powerful enemies. He rendered supreme allegiance to God, whose will was to be obeyed whithersoever it might lead.

The foes of Jesus were sometimes members of his own spiritual household. He and they shared the same religious heritage from the revered past and served the same ancestral Deity. They were as confident as was Jesus that hope for the future depended upon the favor of God. But Jesus' ideals for the remaking of Jewish piety inevitably offended their sense of the proprieties. They deplored his seeming neglect of their sanctified institutions, and their well-trained leaders not unnaturally distrusted the unprofessional activities of a lay reformer. When he fell into disfavor also with the ever suspicious Roman police, who viewed all Jewish agitators as potential revolutionists, his activities were brought to a sudden and tragic close. The Romans crucified him, as they had crucified hundreds of other Jews during the previous period of their rule in Judea.

Jesus' contribution toward the making of religion bore more substantial fruit beyond the limits of strict Judaism.

During his lifetime he had made many friends, especially among the common people. Yet he had not established a clearly differentiated religious sect, like the so-called Zadokites, or the Essene communities. His followers were often a variable and uncertain quantity typical of the unsettled conditions of the times. Those who hung upon his words today, in the hope that this unusual person might give them deliverance from Rome, forsook him tomorrow when he failed to pronounce explicitly against the propriety of paying tribute to Cæsar.

Even those friends who attended Jesus most faithfully were not always clear as to his purposes or fully satisfied with his procedures. They shared his confidence in the coming of the Kingdom of Heaven, they joined him in announcing its advent, and they falteringly pursued the way of life that he advocated and espoused. But they expected him to enact the drama of national deliverance in accordance with their preconceived Jewish notions. Certain of them sought to exact from him a promise of favored positions in the new earthly dominion which they thought he was about to establish (Mark 10: 35-45). And when he entered Jerusalem to celebrate the feast of Passover his ardent admirers hailed him as the prospective restorer of David's régime (Mark 11: 10). People of this temper were hardly in a position to think of Jesus as the founder of a new religion, or to retain under the shock of the crucifixion their confidence in the early dawn of the new age about which he had preached. They quickly disbanded and, being Galileans, returned temporarily disillusioned to the scenes of their former life.

Jesus could not easily be forgotten by those who had been nearest to him through the eventful days of his activity.

He had left with them a memory too fragrant and abiding. Out of this treasure house they presently brought forth things new and old that ultimately welded them together into a new society where the influence of his forceful personality and the revitalizing power of his religious ideals took fresh root and blossomed into an independent religious movement.   In the course of time it acquired the now well-known name of Christianity.   The name was of Gentile origin, but the movement itself, antedating by several years the coining of the new word, inherited its ideals and inspirations directly from Jesus, as his memory was revived by the disciples whom he had won and was perpetuated in their continuing fellowship after they had recovered from their disappointment at his death.

PETER

Among the makers of nascent Christianity in the years immediately following the execution of Jesus, the figure of Simon Peter stands out most conspicuously.   He had been a Galilean fisherman living in Capernaum.   With the impetuosity that characterized him throughout his career, he had given up his business and left his home to become a follower of the teacher from Nazareth.   Yet Peter's had been the tempting voice that would have diverted Jesus from the pathway of the prophetic reformer, doomed to perish at the hands of his enemies.   Could this disciple have had his way, Jesus would have played a triumphant rôle, bringing confusion upon all his enemies (Mark 8: 31-34).   And if that were not to be, Peter was still ready to pledge his fidelity to the bitter end.   But he fell asleep when placed on watch in the garden of Gethsemane on the night of Jesus' arrest.   Although the disciples rushed in terror from the scene, Peter halted his flight long enough to join the rabble at the trial. Then, when called upon to bear testimony, his courage so completely failed him that he denied outright any acquaintance with his master.

The vacillating and impulsive Peter was ultimately to become the generally recognized leader of the new religious society, the rock upon which Jesus was assumed to have founded his church and the keeper of the keys to the Kingdom of Heaven (Matt. 16: 18 f.). There are good reasons for conceding to Peter this distinction. As he had been the last of the disciples to look upon the face of Jesus in the hour of his condemnation to death on the cross, so he too was the first to experience a vision of Jesus risen from among the dead. Peter, overcome by grief and remorse at his momentary weakness in renouncing his master, was transfigured by his latest experience into an ardent champion of a new faith. Associated with him in this effort were a few others who shared his confidence in the reappearances of Jesus.

Peter was no longer troubled with uncertainty about the future. The new day for the faithful in Israel was surely at hand. Jesus' execution had shattered the disciples' vague hopes that he would inaugurate a successful revolution against Rome, but their present belief in his resurrection and ascension to heaven furnished fresh ground for confidence. The victory over evil was to be even more certain and glorious than they had previously imagined, for Jesus was presently to return with heavenly might to establish his kingdom on earth. In the meantime Peter and his companions busied themselves with preaching the same gospel of preparation to which Jesus had devoted his energies, but with an added emphasis on the significance of the Risen One.

In contrast with Jesus' custom of moving about from place to place, Peter and his fellow preachers took up residence in Jerusalem. Evidently they were under the impression that the Day of Judgment was imminent when Jesus would fulfil the prophecy of Malachi: "The Lord whom ye seek will suddenly come to his temple and the messenger of covenant, whom ye desire, behold he cometh. . . . And he will sit as a refiner and purifier of silver, and he will purify the sons of Levi, and refine them as gold and silver, and they shall offer unto Jehovah offerings in righteousness" (Mal. 3: 1-5). Henceforth the heralds of the gospel of reform, who continued the demand made by John the Baptist and Jesus for specialization in righteousness, assembled their disciples in Jerusalem and remained close to the temple ready to receive Christ at his coming. Belief in the risen and glorified Jesus as God's chosen deliverer for the Jewish people now became a cardinal item in the preaching of Peter.

Peter set himself the task of converting the Jewish people in Jerusalem to his new-found faith. It was a Herculean undertaking. No amount of enthusiasm could compensate for the Galilean fisherman's lack of professional training or his crude manner of speech when addressing the religious dignitaries who frequented the Holy City. Yet the preacher, confident that the new day was at hand, labored on with unflagging zeal, buoyed up by an emotional urge that seemed to attest beyond question the arrival of "the last days" when God was to pour out an especial measure of his Holy Spirit upon all true Israelites. Thus throughout a decade or more Peter continued to be the chief spokesman for a comparatively small group of converts residing at Jerusalem. They constituted the earliest Christian church. Peter was in a very real sense its founder, and his firm belief in the risen Jesus was the rock upon which it was built.

Years passed and the judgment day failed to dawn. But Peter and his companions toiled on, winning converts to their cause and consolidating their new society into an organized movement. Opposition from their neighbors only welded them more firmly together and engendered a stronger *esprit de corps*. Their congregation seemed to them to be the true Israel, while their heedless neighbors were a disobedient people. Peter was, as it were, a second Moses charged with the task of leading his kinsmen out of their latest bondage. The Jewish heritage from antiquity was taken to be the rightful possession of Peter's group, which was devout in its loyalty to both the Scriptures and the temple.

At the same time the Petrine congregation soon became keenly conscious of its own distinctiveness. While its structure conformed to the pattern of the Jewish religious assemblies, Peter's memory was drawn upon to enrich its life. The initiatory ceremony of baptism, originally more stressed in the public ministry of John than in that of Jesus, now received new emphasis. Also at regular intervals the devotees broke bread together in memory of the last meal that Jesus had eaten with his disciples. This became a religious rite perpetuating the memory of Jesus' sacrificial death and pledging fidelity to him until his return. But these more external formalities can hardly have been as genuinely significant for the moral and spiritual ideals of the new movement as were Peter's memories of

the precepts, example and inspiring personality of the crucified Nazarene.

Peter was still prominent among the "pillars" of the
Jerusalem church some twenty years after Jesus' death,
when Paul and Barnabas visited the city to attend the
famous gathering described by Paul in the second chapter
of his letter to the Galatians.   In the meantime the church
at Jerusalem had enlarged its missionary outlook to include
the Jewish people in the world at large.   In this enterprise Peter was the recognized leader; he had become the
authentic "apostle to the circumcision" (Gal. 2: 7 f.).
Throughout the intervening years Jews had been constantly
coming and going between Jerusalem and the outlying regions, even as far as Antioch, Alexandria and Rome.   But
how far afield Peter had yet traveled in pursuit of his missionary task is not accurately known.

Peter was still chief among the Christians at Jerusalem
when Paul, about the year 35, paid him a two-weeks visit
(Gal. 1: 18).   Apparently these two notable persons had
not previously met, for Paul's hostility had been directed
against a different congregation under the leadership of
Stephen.   This was a group of Greek-speaking Jews who
had adopted the new teaching about the significance of Jesus
but who, on account of the linguistic barrier, were not at
home in the company headed by Peter, where Aramaic
alone was the common speech.   Probably Paul was familiar
with both languages, but Peter's acquaintance with Greek
was as yet no doubt very limited.   Thus he and his immediate associates had escaped the persecution.   They were
still in Jerusalem carrying on their activity when Paul was
converted on his way to Damascus.   He had not disturbed
the original "apostles" (Gal. 1: 17; Acts 8: 1).

There were, however, other opponents who caused serious inconvenience for Peter and his companions. Although they were devout in their Jewish piety and diligent in their attendance upon ceremonies at the temple, the reverence they paid to the risen Jesus offended the monotheistic scruples of Jewish theologians, while the political authorities looked with suspicion upon the disastrous philosophy of state preached by these ardent believers in an early end of all present governments. In the year 41, the Romans had entrusted the rule of all Palestine to a Jewish prince named Herod Agrippa. He first killed one of Peter's most prominent helpers, James, the son of Zebedee. Later Peter himself was thrown into prison in Jerusalem where he was being held for execution after the celebration of the passover feast in the year 44. But Herod's sudden death altered the situation. As the Jewish historian, Josephus, describes the prince's fatal illness, it would seem that he fell a victim to an acute attack of appendicitis. But to the persecuted Christians it was evident that Herod had been smitten by an angelic avenger, and that Peter's escape from prison had been likewise miraculously effected.

Peter's sphere of operation had been gradually expanding. James, the brother of Jesus, was now the leader in the Jerusalem community. It was for him in particular that Peter left a message with the brethren gathered at the home of John Mark's mother after Peter's escape from prison and his subsequent departure "to another place" (Acts 12: 17). Again, when Paul listed those who were accounted "pillars" in the church at the time of the council at Jerusalem, the name of James preceded that of Peter (Gal. 2: 9). Manifestly, James was in charge of local affairs, while Peter was now the conspicuous leader of the missionary enterprise among his fellow Jews beyond the limits of Jerusalem.

In the meantime Barnabas and Paul had been proclaiming the new faith in the city of Antioch in Syria, as well as in various towns of Cilicia and Asia Minor. At first their efforts had been directed toward the conversion of their numerous Jewish kinsmen residing in these regions. To the congregations in the synagogues the missionaries announced the coming of a new day for Israel, when Jesus would return in triumph from heaven to fulfil for the chosen people God's promises of blessing made to their ancestors. To their faith in God and their observance of his commands revealed in the Scriptures, they needed now to add a profession of allegiance to the risen Jesus as their future Savior. He was God's Anointed One—in Semitic speech, the "Messiah," or, translated into Greek, the "Christ."

Undoubtedly it was a great disappointment to the Christian missionaries to find their Jewish hearers so unresponsive to the new gospel. Relatively few converts were secured, while the preachers were often ejected from the synagogue. But in these ·Jewish assemblies outside of Palestine, where Greek was the language in common use, one not infrequently found Gentiles who had been attracted thither by the noble ethical teachings of the Jews and their more spiritual conception of Deity as revealed in their ancient Scriptures. While these Gentiles hesitated to ally themselves completely with Judaism by accepting the rite of circumcision, which would have identified them with the socially unpopular Jewish group, they nevertheless attended the synagogue and found inspiration in its services. They were welcomed as well-disposed friends who, without becoming full-fledged proselytes, "feared" or "worshiped" the God of the Jews.

Sympathetic Gentiles, who were already familiar with many of the values in Jewish religion, proved more receptive than most Jews were to the message of the Christian missionaries. Barnabas and Paul, when driven from the synagogues, were befriended by these Gentiles, who added belief in Christ to their former interest in Jewish religion. At a Gentile home the new converts assembled to pray to Christ, to participate in the simple rites of the new cult, and to rejoice in their assurances of God's favor. Thus there arose, quite spontaneously, Christian communities outside of Palestine where both Jewish and Gentile converts cherished in common their devotion to Christ and worshiped together under the full glow of a fresh enthusiasm interpreted as a distinct outpouring of the Holy Spirit. Even Christ himself, in unseen but mighty presence, was now felt to be in their midst. Possessed of this assurance, it did not occur to them that further ceremonies, such as circumcision for non-Jewish members of the group, might be necessary to guarantee full participation in future blessings promised by God to the ancient Hebrews.

Peter and James suffered from the handicap of a narrow Palestinian background. They were slow in arriving at the idea of seeking converts beyond the limits of the Jewish race. Paul and Barnabas, who had been Greek-speaking Jews of the Dispersion, found it easier to overstep the bounds of Judaism. Almost by accident, one might say, they had stumbled upon the possibility of a distinctively Gentile mission. But they were ready to make the most of the opportunity, and the success attending their work early convinced them of its propriety. When a Greek was willing to believe on Christ, and thereupon exhibited in his character and zeal those qualities of life that seemed unquestionably to attest God's approval, neither Barnabas nor Paul sought to subject a convert to the law of circumcision as a condition of sharing in the promises that had been made to Abraham when the rite had been instituted (Gen. 17: 10-14). Faith in Christ was all-sufficient for the Gentiles. Any other procedure would have wrecked the social unity of the new congregations.

At the meeting in Jerusalem where the presence of the uncircumcised Greek Christian, Titus, made the issue concrete, both James and Peter agreed that Barnabas and Paul had been acting properly. On the part of James evidently the decision had been in the nature of a concession to a specific situation; it did not mean the recognition of a new universal principle valid for all believers throughout the future course of the new religion's growth. Christianity was still the true Judaism, and the ceremonial establishment of the old dispensation continued to be binding on all of Abraham's descendants who hoped to share in the privileges of the coming Messianic age. The relatively few Greeks who could be gathered into the fold need not submit to the ancient legislation, since God had not established his covenant with their ancestors. But this immunity for Greek Christians was not in the nature of a higher privilege; rather it was a recognition of their inferior status. God's favor had been extended to them only in more recent times, while his concern for the Jews had age-old standing.

Peter had not yet worked his way through the intricacies of the issue, nor did he appreciate its significance for the future of that branch of Christianity which he was largely responsible for founding. James was destined to labor on a few more years in Jerusalem, and to leave behind him a Christian group whose range of vision was so narrowly restricted by its Jewish horizon that an expanding Gentile Christendom would ultimately forget its Palestinian ancestry, or would pronounce heretical the remnants of the Jewish Christian church. But Peter, as the father of Roman Christendom, was to acquire a unique glory elevating him to a position of sainthood and eliciting a reverence second only to that rendered to Christ.

Details of Peter's life during the last decade and a half of his career are tantalizingly scanty. But his fame in the later church is so abundant that his activities must have been exceedingly important. Even apocryphal legend needs some real foundations to insure its prestige; only genuine coins tempt the skill of the counterfeiter. Undoubtedly Peter continued to be a highly significant person in the spread of the Christian movement beyond Palestine, although he rarely emerges from the obscurity that veils the scenes of his activity.

One painful incident connected with Peter's extra-Palestinian career is well known. It occurred at Antioch in Syria soon after the Jerusalem conference at which Paul and Barnabas had secured approval for their custom of admitting uncircumcised Gentiles into the membership of the church. With his usual spontaneity, on arriving at Antioch, Peter participated heartily in the fellowship of the Christian group. It was composed of both Jewish and Gentile converts. As yet the "church" was simply a congregation assembling regularly for friendly intercourse and worship at the home of some member who might be so fortunately circumstanced as to be able to provide entertainment. Probably this host would often be a Gentile convert, whose hospitality was extended to the entire brotherhood irrespective of racial inheritance. Into this mixed society's life Peter had entered without hesitation when he first came to Antioch.

News of Peter's conduct quickly traveled to Jerusalem. James was horrified; there had been a grave misunderstanding. Gentiles might properly hope to enter the Kingdom of God simply through the exercise of faith in Christ, but Jewish Christians had as a peculiar possession sacred guaranties from antiquity that they could ill afford to ignore. God's favor for them had been established long ago in the covenant of circumcision and the revelation of the divine will regarding clean and unclean foods. This high privilege belonged to Jews only, and its value was enhanced rather than abrogated when one went on to the more complete fulfilment of the divine will by believing in Christ. Gentiles, less highly favored by God, were not children of the ancient covenant and hence their opportunity to please Deity lay in the more recent privilege of accepting Christ as Savior. They could claim nothing from God on the basis of promises given to and covenants established with his chosen people.

Conversely, Jewish Christians inherited from the past the fulness of God's promises and the obligation to keep all his revealed laws. Uncircumcised Gentiles, even when Christians, were not of this privileged group. Both they and their food were still "kosher," and, therefore, the Jewish Christian rendered himself ceremonially unclean when he "ate with the Gentiles" in the church at Antioch. Peter as well as Barnabas had unwittingly overlooked this fine point of logic until James, on hearing of their action, had dispatched messengers from Jerusalem to warn them of their improper conduct. This warning proved effective. Much to Paul's disgust, the main body of the Jewish Christians in the Antioch church, including even Barnabas, retracted. Gentile converts were not denied a place in Christianity, nor were they asked to submit to the ceremonial regulations of the Law, but Christian Jews ought not to ignore any part of that sacred inheritance. When they associated on an equality with their Gentile brethren at a church banquet, they had violated God's command. James would have two denominations of Christians on Gentile soil—the closed communion of the "kosher" group and the open communion of the "goim."

Paul's vigorous condemnation of Peter's conduct has been preserved in one of the New Testament books (Gal. 2: 11-21). Unfortunately, no counter statement from Peter has survived; he was not, like Paul, given to much writing of letters during the decade following their disagreement at Antioch. For events in the closing years of Peter's career one is left mainly to conjecture. His dominating influence in Antioch, over even so significant a person as Barnabas, is evident from Paul's language. Similarly, incidental references in Paul's correspondence with the Corinthians testify to the prestige of Peter's name on Greek soil. Though he may never have visited Corinth, there were persons in the church of that place who admired his type of Christianity (I Cor. 1:12; 3:22). The Corinthians also knew that Peter and his wife were traveling missionaries who regularly received support from the communities which they served (I Cor. 9:5). True to his duty as "apostle to the circumcision," he probably devoted his energies to evangelizing Jews in the Dispersion. He must have acquired a measure of competence in the use of everyday Greek as he pursued this task.

Peter was always amenable to the educative influence of new experiences. Often his first reactions were hasty, but he was ready to profit from the sobering effects of subsequent reflection. By this process of development he had succeeded in revising some of his earlier opinions and attitudes while associated with Jesus, and the same capacity for readjustment placed him in a position of leadership among the disciples after the crucifixion. This quality of character is not likely to have failed him in that critical moment at Antioch when he found himself a leader in the Christian group that broke with Paul. For the moment, the logic of James seemed invincible to Peter; if Jewish Christians were to participate in the fulfilment of God's promises they must remain true to every detail of the covenant made with the chosen people. But the practical difficulties of establishing a mixed Christian society on Gentile soil by adhering thus literalistically to ancient Jewish legislation were not as yet fully appreciated by Peter. He had new lessons to learn from later experiences.

The natural place in Peter's personal development for readjustment of his views on the propriety of eating at table with converted Gentiles came after his visit to Antioch, as he pursued his evangelistic labors southward in Syria. When a converted Gentile, like the pious Cornelius, wished to entertain the Jewish Christian preacher it did seem to the hungry Peter absurd for him to call common or unclean one who was so manifestly pleasing to God. Scriptural injunctions regarding clean and unclean contacts were not to be set aside, but they needed reinterpretation in view of God's new revelation of himself and his power to converted Gentiles. The purity of the table would have to be safeguarded by moral and culinary proprieties. Unconverted persons who frequented pagan feasts or defiled themselves with harlots must not be present, nor should meat be served from strangled animals which had died with the blood still in the carcass. But when these concessions to Jewish scruples had been made, the table of the converted Gentile was no longer taboo for the conscientious Christian of Jewish ancestry (Acts 15: 20).

This solution of an acute social problem saved the Jewish church on Gentile soil from a repetition of the embarrassment that had arisen at Antioch. To Peter and Barnabas, rather than to Paul, must be given the credit for resolving the difficulty. Their policy was fundamentally different from that of Paul, who would make the whole question of clean and unclean meats an affair of the individual's conscience in relation to the needs of the weak brother (I Cor. 10: 23-33). But Peter was more institutionally minded. He wanted an established rule of conduct that would preserve the sanctity of Jewish tradition without seeming to sacrifice the values of Christian liberty, while at the same time it would preserve the integrity of the new Christian society. His situation was similar to that of the educated Indian Christian today who points with satisfaction to the fact that the annual banquet of his Christian college is attended by both converted and non-Christian Brahmans. But inquiry will reveal that the food has been prepared by a Brahman chef.

While substantial literary evidence for Peter's continued activity on Gentile soil is wanting, his great importance for the further development of the Christian movement is beyond question. He and his fellow laborers sponsored a type of Christianity that grew side by side with the Pauline churches and ultimately transcended them in the popular esteem of the Roman world. The Petrine communities gave precedence to the authority of the Scriptures, in contrast with the antilegalism and spiritual individualism of Paul. On this Jewish foundation they reared an ecclesiastical institution fortified by an accumulating Christian tradition and a growing apostolic authority within which even the militant Paul was later to be given an honored place.

Peter's career closed with the church's gaze still steadfastly fixed upon the hoped-for day whose coming he had heralded. Small groups of the faithful, who awaited eagerly Jesus' return, had been assembled at the chief centers of life about the Mediterranean, even in the city of Rome itself. As yet these gospel preachers had been unable to envisage the larger task of winning to Christ the great masses of the population and establishing a religious institution to survive even the downfall of the mighty Roman Empire. They were struggling to rescue the few prepared for the new kingdom of God to be inaugurated by the appearing of the triumphant Christ. In the meantime his followers were despised, afflicted and slain by their demonic foes. Since their victory was not an affair of this world, present calamities brought them no sense of defeat. The hour of affliction only heightened their confidence in ultimate victory.

That Peter died in Rome about the year 64, executed among the Christians who suffered under Nero, is as probable a conjecture as can be ventured in the absence of substantial data of either a negative or positive character. At least no other Christian community ever claimed the honor of enshrining his mortal remains. It is quite unlikely that he was the first Christian to reach Rome, but no other ancient Christian community represents more consistently his spirit and temper, or the type of Christianity which he had advocated. Paul's epistle addressed to the church at Rome shortly before the year 60, reveals there a form of the Christian religion that had been looked at askance by this apostle ever since he had experienced the crisis at Antioch a decade before. Rome was already a "Petrine" church, whether it owed its distinctive character to Peter himself or to other laborers of like heritage and interests.

CHAPTER II

CHAMPIONS OF WORLD-
EVANGELIZATION

Gentiles first learned about Christianity from its Jewish representatives. Missionaries like Peter and Barnabas remained firmly rooted in Judaism. Although they welcomed converts from heathenism, they aimed chiefly at assembling congregations composed of Jews who had accepted Jesus as Messiah. The consummation of the Christian enterprise would be realized through God's miraculous restoration of Palestine to his chosen people when they had turned to Christ. Toward the realization of this end the missionaries were laboring among their kinsmen in the Jewish Dispersion, while incidentally they were offering Gentiles an opportunity to participate in the privileges designed by God for the Hebrews and their descendants. A long time was yet to elapse before the makers of Christianity would realize that they were building a world-church, with a membership predominantly or exclusively Gentile.

PAUL

Paul was the most conspicuous leader in the initial stages of Christianity's spread among Gentiles. His indefatigable labors, his remarkable originality, and his unswerving devotion to duty compel admiration. Respect for the man and appreciation of his work may lead one to overlook those antecedent conditions which have to be observed if the full significance of Paul's contribution to the expansion of Christianity is to be correctly understood. He built upon the work of predecessors, both Jewish and Christian.

Religious leaders among the Jews of the Dispersion had for generations been zealous to win Gentiles. They were welcomed to the services in the synagogues, where they heard the Scriptures read and expounded in the Greek language of everyday life. They were admonished to forsake the folly and wickedness of idolatry for the worship of the Hebrew God, and they were invited to adopt the moral ideals and religious customs of Judaism. When willing to take the final step in accepting the Mosaic rites, Gentiles could become fully initiated members of the Jewish religion. Even if they stopped short of this ultimate goal, they were still an object of friendly concern and solicitous attention for the broader-minded rabbis ever desirous of bringing worthy Gentiles into the Jewish fold. Probably this had been the atmosphere in which Paul grew up in the city of Tarsus. When he entered upon training for the rabbinate as a life-work, undoubtedly he cherished an ambition to convert through his ministry a goodly number of Gentiles to the Jewish faith.

Paul had been a precocious youth, if he has not misjudged his own attainments. He says that no other young man of the same age had progressed so rapidly in religious studies or been more zealous for the ancestral faith. This ardor had led him to attack those groups of his kinsmen who revered the crucified Jesus (Gal. 1: 13 f.). Where Paul found them, or under whose leadership they had been assembled, he does not state. Apart from a mention of Arabia and its principal city, Damascus, Paul makes no reference to the scene of his activities during the first three years immediately following his conversion to Christianity. But he does clearly imply that his persecution had not disturbed the apostolic company in Jerusalem; he did not take the trouble even to seek instruction from Peter before setting out upon the new task of preaching Christ "among the Gentiles" (Gal. 1:15-17).

The Christians with whom Paul first came into conflict were Greek-speaking converts from among the Jews of the Dispersion, who no doubt were even more earnest than ever to bring Gentiles into the better Judaism which now they believed themselves to represent. Perhaps they were persons of Stephen's type. He is, indeed, hardly more than a name today; history has not recorded the details of his career except to glorify him as the first martyr to follow in the footsteps of Jesus. But the shadowy figure of Stephen is sufficiently distinct to shed a good deal of light upon the conditions leading up to Paul's conversion, as well as upon the type of activity to which he thereafter devoted his energies.

One can easily imagine how Paul, an ardent young student preparing himself for religious leadership among the Jews of the Dispersion, would have felt on first hearing a Christian preacher like Stephen. Under immediate inspiration of the Spirit the speaker seemed to claim for himself an authority superior to the revered traditions of the fathers, if not indeed to the sacred Scriptures. This attitude was a serious reflection upon the sanctity of the professional school's curriculum—a slur that a clever pupil like Paul, proud of his grades, was sure to resent. More offensive still was the theological menace. Jesus, a crucified man, was alleged to be at the right hand of God in heaven where he held a position of lordship almost rivaling that of the supreme Deity. This, thought Paul, would be a most pernicious doctrine to propagate among Gentiles, who were especially susceptible to the worship of deified heroes and princes. The central note in orthodox Jewish propaganda had been an appeal for worship of the one and only God. But if the Christian error, masquerading as true Judaism, were permitted to continue, it would prove a curse to the heathen and an embarrassment to Jews. Paul's plans for a life-work were being endangered.

The depth of Paul's feelings is evidenced by the violence of his action. On his own showing, he had been a vicious persecutor (Gal. 1: 13; I Cor. 15: 9). Later he lamented this conduct, but he never intimated that his motives had been insincere or that he had acted contrary to his honest convictions. Believing that God had summoned him to this task, he would follow duty to the bitter end. The Christians whom he attacked justified their faith in Christ on the ground that the crucified Jesus had appeared alive again, showing himself to Peter and others in the early days of the new movement's history. But the last of these appearances had occurred months, or perhaps years, before; and Paul was not ready to credit second-hand testimony on so unusual and important a matter. Then suddenly he experienced a fresh emotional upheaval resulting in the complete reversal of his former conduct. As Paul phrased it, God intervened to stay the hand of the persecutor by granting him a belated vision of the Risen One. As Jesus had appeared to Peter and his companions in earlier days, so now he made a final appearance also to Paul (I Cor. 15: 8; Gal. 1: 15 f.).

Paul, converted, was the same ardent protagonist of Christianity that he had previously been of Judaism. His transformation had been complete. Those aspects of the new religion that had incensed him most as an enemy, were now the items about which his interest and loyalty chiefly centered. He yielded supreme allegiance to belief in the resurrection and the consequent lordship of Jesus, who would presently return to inaugurate the Kingdom of God. In the meantime Paul also proclaimed the primacy of the Holy Spirit as a guide superior in authority to all rabbinical traditions. From the point of view of present-day psychology, this change in Paul's attitude awakens curiosity and invites speculation regarding the nature of the occurrence. But one may easily be misled at this point by too much psychologizing in the modern vein.

Paul's understanding of the situation was simple enough. Consumed with zeal for his God, he had thrown himself vigorously into the persecution of the Christian congregations. For a man of his highly emotional and conscientious nature, every overmastering impulse was instantly felt to be a divine command. If the result proved distressing to his emotions, former convictions could be properly revised, not by the reflective processes of human thinking, but only by the immediate interference of Deity. When Paul discovered that his restless quest for divine approval had not been quieted, but only further unsettled, by contact with Christians, who stoutly withstood the persecutor and confidently reaffirmed their faith in the risen and glorified Jesus, God's intervention was needed to rectify the situation. Paul would take no credit to himself for abandoning his earlier course of action, although it may have been leading him into ever deepening perplexity. It is true that he found escape by turning to the living Christ in whom Christians rejoiced with full assurance even in the hour of death. Paul might have envied them their spiritual satisfaction, but it did not occur to him that he might on his own initiative voluntarily choose the more desirable way. This was not in accord with his habit of mind. Only God could give him his heart's desire. And God did.

"God revealed his Son to me that I might preach him to the Gentiles." Paul's gospel had been given to him "through revelation of Jesus Christ." It now seemed to him that from the day of his birth he had been divinely set apart for his evangelistic task. Important decisions in his later career were determined "by revelation." "Visions and revelations" furnished him guidance throughout his life. When this distinctive aspect of the Pauline psychology has been duly recognized, much that might otherwise be unintelligible in the Apostle's mental and spiritual processes becomes readily understood. He possessed strong convictions, great firmness of character, an exceedingly sensitive conscience, an abiding readiness to scrutinize his own motives, and no slight ability to adjust his actions to the necessities or proprieties of changing circumstances. Few if any of his Christian contemporaries exhibited an equal capacity for making themselves "all things to all men." But these qualities, so significant for his success as an advocate of the new religion, were not matters of human preference. Paul resented vigorously any suspicion that his primary aim was to please men. His impulses, choices, decisions, and enterprises, however prudently shaped by the instructive experiences of practical living, were believed to be dictated by the will of God. This was a cardinal item in Paul's psychology.

The first decade and a half of Paul's Christian activity is a relatively obscure period. During these years he composed no letters that have survived, and in his comparatively abundant correspondence after the year 50, he referred only incidentally to earlier events in his career. He had lived in and about Damascus for three years. Evidently his preaching there, as so often in places where he labored, proved disturbing to the peace of the community. Hostility between Jewish and Christian groups led to riotous disturbances, with which the local Gentile police had no sympathy. Since Christians were the smaller unit in the conflict, the authorities readily laid upon them the blame for all disturbances and sought to eliminate trouble by arresting Christian leaders. When the situation had become thus acute in Damascus, Paul effected his escape through the kindness of friends who let him down from a window in the wall of the city (II Cor. 11: 32 f.).

Violence was a favorite instrument used for preserving order in ancient society. Measured by modern standards, justice was often blind and very rarely was it seasoned with mercy. The Jewish communities, even in the Dispersion, maintained the whipping-post in connection with the synagogue, where the thirty-nine (forty) lashes prescribed by Jewish law for specified irregularities were administered to offenders. Five times Paul received this punishment from his kinsmen (II Cor. 11:24). Death by stoning was to be inflicted upon one guilty of blasphemy, a penalty which the strict Jew conscientiously believed Christians deserved, who infringed upon the supremacy of God by elevating Jesus to the divine sphere and by confessing their belief in his lordship. Undoubtedly this law had been invoked by Paul in his persecution of Christians. It was normal procedure for the Jews to stone Stephen when he blasphemously declared that he saw Jesus standing at God's right hand in heaven (Acts 7: 57 f.). Alleged profanation of the Sabbath, or persistent disregard of the laws respecting clean and unclean meats, merited a similarly harsh punishment. Paul had once been caught in the net of Jewish justice and received the extreme penalty of stoning, but he had survived the ordeal (II Cor. 11:25; Acts 14:19 f.). On another occasion he escaped by appealing to his rights as a Roman citizen, but he was left to lie for years in prison, a victim of tardy Roman judicial procedures.

Notwithstanding the tremendous odds against him, Paul persisted in his evangelistic activities. After leaving Damascus he spent two weeks in Jerusalem with Peter, and then moved on into "the regions of Syria and Cilicia," where he worked for over a decade. During these rather shadowy years of his career, the city of Antioch in Syria seems to have been his principal place of residence and Barnabas was his most distinguished co-laborer. Since it was their custom to support themselves by their own earnings, rather than to receive a living from the congregations to which they ministered (I Cor. 9: 6), the range of their activities was necessarily restricted by economic conditions. Toward the close of this period they made a notable missionary tour northward into central Asia Minor. One would like to know more exactly what the specific conditions of his health were that brought about Paul's presence among the Galatians when first he preached in their territory. It would seem that he had gone from the low-lying coast lands into the higher country because of "an infirmity of the flesh," and while seeking the recovery of health had embraced a new opportunity to spread the gospel (Gal. 4: 13).

On returning to Antioch in Syria he was confronted by fresh troubles. Conservative Jewish scruples about admitting uncircumcised Gentiles into the church had spread from Jerusalem to the wider mission field. Although this home base supplied no funds, its prestige could not be ignored and its suspicions needed to be allayed. The result was the notable gathering at Jerusalem, where Barnabas, Paul and Titus presented themselves to the mother church of all Christendom. On discovering that a decision favorable to the visitors was not likely to be rendered at a meeting of the entire congregation, they resorted to a conference with the "pillars," especially James, Peter and John. The desired concessions were granted, on condition that the mission churches should help finance the home church! It might be worth while for missionaries today to try a similar method of placating troublesome home boards. In Galatians 2: 1-10, Paul has given a vivid description of his procedure.

Paul's delight over the outcome of the meeting at Jerusalem was short-lived. The rift with Peter and Barnabas at Antioch followed almost immediately. The position maintained by Paul in this disagreement was one of his most valuable original contributions to the expanding Christian movement. Paul had no desire to shed outright his abundant Jewish heritages. In fact, personally he never did. But his battle royal with his Christian opponents at Antioch established a principle of the utmost significance for Christianity's further development. For the moment the issue seemed to be primarily a question of practical procedure. Peter conceded Gentiles the right to membership in the church but denied them social and ritual equality with Jewish converts. Even when Peter modified his practice, the new regulations regarding the type of food and companionship proper for a mixed Christian community were fundamentally in the temper of Jewish legalism. True religion, although modified to meet new social conditions, was made essentially the privilege of a chosen racial or national group.

On the other hand, Paul's position cleared the way for Christianity to transcend all national or racial limitations by stressing the all-sufficiency of an individual's voluntary act in accepting Christ as his Savior. Religion was thus a strictly personal affair, and its privileges were equally accessible to persons of any race or land. Paul had sensed, consciously or unconsciously, the degree to which the demand for a religion free from older restrictions to clans or localities was increasing in the cosmopolitan society of the Roman Empire. By making the act of personal belief the only prerequisite for salvation, Paul opened wide the door for Christianity to become in time the most effectual religion in the Roman world.

The congregation at Antioch was no longer in full sympathy with Paul. Henceforth that church could not remain his home base; sympathies there were predominantly on the side of Barnabas and Peter. Therefore Paul wandered farther afield, moving up through Asia Minor and on to Macedonia and Greece. During his next decade of work his chief places of residence were to be the preëminently Greek cities of Corinth and Ephesus. Here he supported himself by laboring at his trade—the preparation of skins or cloth used for tent coverings—and preached his gospel to people whom he encountered in his ordinary daily contacts. In the drifting population of these important centers he also occasionally met Christian travelers and by the aid of available means of communication exercised a pastoral care, often by correspondence, over several congregations.

During this period his chief extant letters were composed.

It was a great moment in Paul's life when he passed over from Asia to Europe. Barnabas was no longer his helper. He was accompanied, however, by new assistants in the persons of Silas and Timothy; and probably it was about this time that he made the acquaintance of Luke, "the beloved physician." The small band of travelers moved in a leisurely way through the Macedonian towns of Philippi, Thessalonica, and Berea, thence to Athens in Greece and on to Corinth, where Paul settled down for a more permanent stay. Jews were less numerous in these regions than in Syria and Asia, but they were sufficiently in evidence to create the usual troubles for the Christian preacher. The converts won in these new territories were, however, mainly from among Gentiles. Paul left behind him in Philippi and Thessalonica groups of disciples to whom he later wrote interesting letters. In Athens he was less successful, but at Corinth he assembled one of the most important churches in the eastern Mediterranean area. Here he was able to support himself for several months, while he preached Christianity in this thriving commercial center.

The message of Paul underwent some significant changes in his new Gentile environment. At Thessalonica he had made the customary missionary appeal to Gentiles, admonishing his hearers to abandon idolatry for the service of the true God of the Hebrew people. To this Jewish teaching he added the distinctively Christian injunction to await the coming of Jesus from heaven to raise the dead and deliver the righteous from the terrors of the judgment day (I Thess. 1:9 f.). "Forsake idols and prepare for resurrection and judgment by believing on Christ" appear to have been the requirements chiefly stressed by Paul in the

early days of his preaching on Greek soil. His success had
not been remarkable. At Athens, the learned center of
the ancient world, his university sermon to the philosophers
was a dismal failure. He arrived in Corinth discouraged
and perplexed. He was not sure that he knew how to
present Christ appealingly to the Greeks; it was with a
sense of weakness, and in fear and much trembling, that he
began preaching in Corinth (I Cor. 2:3).

His fears were needless. A new decision regarding the
form of his preaching had emerged out of his perplexity.
The attack upon idolatry was not to be abandoned, but it
would no longer be a chief point of stress in his sermons.
Nor would he dwell especially upon resurrection and judgment, although this item in Christian faith was to remain
unchanged. Rather, Paul adopted a new strategy: "I determine not to know anything among you, save Jesus Christ
and him crucified." The preacher would present the new
faith as a divine hero-centered mystery, attested not by
the convincing power of words but by a demonstration of
God's spirit and power in the emotional experiences of the
convert (I Cor. 2:4 f.). In making this decision Paul
truly perceived the distinctive religious needs and interests
of his Corinthian audience.

Popular religion among Gentiles of the lower classes in
this period was less a matter of doctrinal or moral instruction and more an experience of divine dynamic acquired by
the devotee through voluntary attachment to a saving deity.
This divinity was believed to have experienced in a life upon
earth the acutest sufferings to which flesh is heir, even death
itself. But ultimately all hostile powers had been thwarted
and the powerful god or goddess was henceforth the peculiar friend of those who attached themselves to the cult of

the victorious hero or heroine. Suitable initiation ceremonies provided an emotional experience of intimate union
between the worshiper and his deity, while ritualistic performances repeated at stated seasons furnished opportunity
for renewing one's consciousness of divine uplift and protection. Long before Paul's day various religions of this
type had been popular among Greeks, who called these
cults "mysteries."

If Paul traveled by land from Athens to Corinth he
passed close by Eleusis, the seat of the widely revered mystery cult of Demeter. Every native wayfarer could testify
to the incalculable blessing bestowed upon mankind by
Demeter in her gratitude for the successful escape of her
daughter, Persephone, from the machinations of the god
of the nether regions. Persons who had passed through
the moving experiences of initiation were not at liberty to
reveal the details of the sacred rites, but they gladly bore
witness to the personal religious value of the ceremonies.
Perhaps another fellow-traveler told of his satisfaction at
having participated recently in the mysteries of Dionysus,
when in ecstatic frenzy the worshiper had eaten the warm
flesh of the slaughtered victim and had felt himself filled
with the god. The devotee thus became an "in-god" man—
a man in whom the god dwelt. Still other companions
might speak of heroic helpers like Herakles or Asklepios,
who, having triumphantly endured great trials, were now
generous in their help for mortals. A few miles beyond
Corinth, at Epidauros, there was a famous sanitarium
whither invalids from all parts of the world came seeking
help from a divinity who had himself once passed successfully through even the gates of death. Possibly some
chance acquaintance of Paul's on the way to Corinth may

have suggested that he visit Epidauros to seek from Asklepios the removal of the apostle's "thorn in the flesh." This divine healer was reputed to have relieved all sorts of bodily infirmities for those who sought his assistance. He might be willing to help Paul.

One may easily imagine how revolting this suggestion would have been to Paul. His Jewish disdain for polytheism, combined with his loyalty to Christ, rendered impossible any admiration on Paul's part for the much belauded Gentile gods and heroes. Their images were nothing but senseless blocks of wood, stone or metal, while all their sacred rites were the devices of wicked demons. Paul would have no traffic with demons, even for the purpose of exorcising from his own flesh the "angel of Satan" that constantly afflicted him. He reasoned that the demonic infection remained in his body, not because of Christ's inability to expel the evil spirit, but because its presence served a useful function in maintaining the apostle's emotional equilibrium (II Cor. 12: 7). Christ was all-sufficient for every proper need. The Greeks had been deluded into believing that there are "many gods and many lords," but Paul knew that there is only one God, who is the creator of all things, and one Lord who is the crucified and risen Jesus revered by the Christians (I Cor. 8: 4-6).

Paul was convinced that Christ was sufficient even for all the religious needs of the Greeks. He was, indeed, their only hope. It was the supreme duty of the missionary to make this fact evident through an effective presentation of the Christian gospel. This was a heaven-assigned task for Paul; woe would overtake him if he ceased to preach Christ. As he acquired a deeper insight into the characteristic quests of the Greeks, and learned more about the types of satisfaction derived by them from the worship of their popular divinities, he became more skilful in expounding the full range of Christ's sufficiency.

Pauline Christianity in Gentile lands carried forward abundant heritages from its Jewish antecedents. The apostle's sentimental attachment to the Hebrew race never wavered, nor did he venture to envisage a future day when the new religion would proclaim utter rejection of Jews in favor of a purely Gentile church. As he viewed the gospel tree, it was rooted in Jewish soil and would bear its fruits in the coming Messianic age realized after the Jewish model. Missionary service to the Gentiles was only a temporary phase of the Christian program. But Paul's work among Greeks, especially at Corinth and Ephesus, was so effective in transplanting the gospel tree to foreign soil and in grafting upon this exotic stem so many fruit-bearing shoots from Gentile saplings, that he has sometimes been called a new founder of Christianity. Perhaps he deserves more credit in this respect than he would himself have been willing to admit.

To a considerable extent Paul became the creator of a new form of Christianity. This fact is apparent from the outstanding features of his religion as revealed in his correspondence during the years following the beginnings of his work at Corinth. While he perpetuated the authority of the Hebrew Scriptures and proclaimed in primitive Jewish Christian fashion the imminent coming of Christ, he also stressed faith in Christ as the hero who by his victory over death had become the author of a new "mystery" religion. The baptismal rite of initiation was not only a pledge of repentance, but symbolized or effected mystical union with the hero-savior and birth into a new life. The baptized believer was a "new creation in Christ Jesus"; henceforth Christ was in him, the hope of glory. The indwelling divinity, as Lord, Christ, Holy Spirit, was a continuous presence that supplied perpetual guidance for the individual and the religious community. The Spirit assigned various duties to officiating members of the congregation, inspired the prophet to address the assembly, prompted the singing of hymns, and induced the ecstatic utterances of those who spoke "in tongues." The Lord's Supper called to mind the last meal eaten by Jesus with his disciples, and revived the hope of his return. This memorial and anticipatory significance of the rite perpetuated primitive Jewish Christian interest, but the Pauline churches added a new note with a sacramental emphasis. It was a communion of the blood and body of Christ, as the similar rite in the Greek cults was a communion with demons.

The Christianity of the Pauline churches had taken a long stride forward in the direction of becoming a genuinely indigenous religion on Gentile soil. While this outcome was gratifying to Paul, in so far as it represented the recognition of Christ's full sufficiency for the believer, in contrast with the Jewish Christian emphasis on a legally regulated religion, in other respects it frequently caused the apostle great anxiety. His moral sensitivity was often shocked by the conduct of his converts. Gentiles lacked the momentum of the ethical ideals and training that Paul had inherited from his Jewish ancestry. Greek Christians could not always be trusted to "walk by the Spirit"; they needed a more objective guide. This guidance Paul tried to furnish by personal contacts, or by correspondence. His letters are full of warnings and commands, urging the cultivation of worthier moral attainments. The Christian faith had come to be thoroughly at home among Gentiles, but Christian discipline was still in its infancy.

Paul was prevented by circumstances beyond his control from carrying his task through to completion. After his period of labor at Corinth and Ephesus, he visited Jerusalem where his arrest and subsequent imprisonment at Cæsarea resulted in two years of comparative inactivity (Acts, Chaps. 21-26). The eventful sea voyage to Rome was followed by two more years of incarceration.. Beyond this date his activities are veiled in much obscurity. Whether he secured release, only to be later arrested and executed at Rome, or was put to death as a climax to his first imprisonment, are questions that cannot be positively answered today. But in any event it is certain that he ultimately won the martyr's crown at Rome, probably in the same outburst of hostility against Christians that had led shortly before to the execution of Peter.

Some thirty years later the church at Rome, writing to the Pauline congregation in Corinth, composed the following brief but irenic eulogy to the memory of the two great rivals: "Let us fix our gaze upon the good apostles. Peter, a victim of wicked jealousy, endured not one or two but abundant labors, and so by a martyr's death attained his glorious reward. Paul, a victim of jealousy and strife, made plain the prize of patient endurance. Seven times in prison-chains, forced to flee, stoned, having preached in the East and the West, he received the distinguished glory due his faith. When he had taught righteousness throughout all the world, having gone to its western limit (Rome) and borne his testimony before the rulers, he then departed from the world and went to his holy reward, a most illustrious example of patient endurance."

The Evangelists

Both Peter and Paul had numerous companions. Many of them were younger men who, no doubt, carried on missionary propaganda years after the older leaders had moved off the stage. One would like to be able to follow day by day the doings of John Mark, Apollos, Titus, Timothy, Luke, Silas, Agabus, Philip of Cæsarea with his four prophetess-daughters, Judas of Antioch, Lydia of Thyatira, Aquila, Prisca, Zenas the lawyer, Dionysius of Athens, Jason of Thessalonica, Sopater of Berea, Aristarchus and Secundus of Thessalonica, Tychicus and Trophimus of Ephesus, Gaius of Derbe, Archippus, Onesimus, Philemon, Epaphras, Justus, Erastus, Artemas, Demas, Sosthenes, and a host of others now unknown even by name.

The persons responsible for the expansion of Christianity during the last quarter of the first century are today largely a nameless generation of leaders. No substantial body of biographical data has survived from that period of history. Yet under the guidance of now forgotten champions the new religion continued to widen its influence and consolidate its strength, especially among Gentiles. Its advocates were content to lose themselves in the cause they served, leaving to posterity the rich heritage of their labors. They are known by their fruits rather than by their specific names.

After 66 A.D. Christians in Palestine were well-nigh overwhelmed by a flood of adverse circumstances. Although they had refused to join with their Jewish compatriots in the disastrous revolution against Rome, they suffered bitterly from its consequences. About the year 69, as the Roman soldiers closed in upon Jerusalem, the Christian congregation withdrew to Pella beyond the Jordan. Its outstanding leader, James the brother of Jesus, and possibly also John the son of Zebedee, had already fallen a victim to the violence of enemies. In any event, John was no longer a member of the Palestinian Christian community. Later tradition reports that the group was without formally recognized leadership until Symeon, a cousin of Jesus, was elected to supervise its affairs. It is not likely that the church had been able to reëstablish itself in Jerusalem during the distressing years following the capture of the city by the Romans, and henceforth it quickly faded out of the picture. The future of the Christian movement lay with its propagators on Gentile soil.

Both Jewish and Gentile converts labored together at the new task of world-evangelization. Recent events had necessitated some radical readjustments in outlook and activity. The prospect of persuading Jews to accept Christ grew constantly less promising, while Roman resentment at the rebellious temper of the Jewish people in Palestine made it increasingly desirable for Christianity to counteract as rapidly as possible the popular assumption that it was only a new Jewish cult. Yet the values of ancient Hebrew religion preserved in the ancient Scriptures were too enormous to be sacrificed in the process of Christianity's transition to the Gentile world. The effective alternative was to assume that God, having deprived the Jews of their birthright, had willed that it should become the proper possession of Gentile Christendom. This inference seemed abundantly confirmed by the disaster that had overtaken the Jewish religion in the destruction of its temple at Jerusalem by the Romans in 70 A.D. Further confirmation of God's rejection of the Jews was seen in the bitter enmity of the synagogues in the Dispersion to the growing Christian churches.

Christian leaders also needed new instruments for use in establishing and giving dignity to the Gentile churches. At the outset the missionaries on Gentile soil hardly seem to have realized the full extent to which the heroic career of the earthly Jesus could be used with persuasive power among Greeks and Romans. Peter and Paul had centered their attention so preëminently on the risen Christ, presently to return in triumph to inaugurate in Palestine the true Kingdom of God, that the full significance of Jesus' life on earth had not been given due attention. This defect was corrected in the next generation. Christian leaders now became more diligent in calling to mind the exemplary life of Jesus, his marvelous teachings, his mighty works, his unique favor with God, his fulfilment of ancient prophecies, his care in training future workers for his cause, and his provisions for the founding of a new and continuing religious society. The outcome of these labors in fortifying the missionary propaganda ultimately crystallized into a body of Christian writings known today as "gospels," which in their present form were composed in the Greek language between the years 70 and 100.

The contribution of the "evangelists," as the writers of the New Testament gospels are commonly called, toward the making of Christianity was tremendously important. This fact renders it all the more regrettable that biographical information regarding these Christian leaders, who assembled and recorded traditions about the life and work of Jesus, is so exceedingly scanty. Even their several names cannot now be known with certainty. Unlike Paul, no one of them took pains to subscribe his signature to his book.

They seem to have had no itch for the distinction of author-ship; their message carried authority in its own right since it was the common possession of the worshiping congregations. In later times, when the church desired to give these books a more formal authority, it prefaced them with titles ascribing their composition severally to Mark, Matthew, Luke, and John. Today the accuracy of this surmise, especially in the case of "Matthew" and "John," has become widely questioned.

Let the evangelists remain nameless if we must. They nevertheless represent a very significant group of anonymous toilers who gathered up from the past and recast for immediate use an extensive body of missionary material peculiarly serviceable to the new religion. Their creative labors marked a distinct advance in Christianity's progress toward world-evangelization.

Henceforth the leaders of the church perceived that God had never intended Christianity to be espoused mainly by Jews. Their rejection of the Christian message had been clearly foreshadowed by their hostile attitude toward Jesus. Nor were Gentile converts to be brought under bondage to the legal prescriptions of the rabbis, for Jesus had shown himself superior to all such enactments. He had declared himself lord even of the Sabbath and had pronounced all meats clean. While he had not rescinded the ancient and revered Mosaic dispensation, but had affirmed the validity of its every jot or tittle, his authority transcended even that of Moses and prescribed in addition a new and higher rule of living. The sacred Scriptures of the Hebrews were the rightful possession of Christendom, wherein the predictions of the prophets found fulfilment and the ancient law received its correct interpretation. Thus the asperities that had caused friction between Peter and Paul were softened in the interests of a Gentile Christianity that would perpetuate the entire Scriptural heritage from Judaism and at the same time expound its meaning in accordance with the necessities of the church. It was now believed that Jesus himself, while yet on earth, had authorized this procedure.

By the end of the first century the makers of Gentile Christendom had progressed remarkably in converting—perverting, Jews would have said—the ancient Scriptures into a specifically Gentile Christian book. Failure to win large numbers of Jewish converts no longer caused serious concern, since all the promises of God to Abraham and his descendants were now to be fulfilled in favor of Gentile believers on Christ. But less progress had been made in Hellenizing Christendom's outlook upon its future task. The Jewish Christian hope of Christ's early coming, miraculously to establish the Kingdom of God and destroy his enemies in the purging fire of judgment, was still fondly cherished. This catastrophic event was to be longer delayed than either Peter or Paul had imagined. But as yet the task of a world-evangelization was not thought to be the building up of a cosmopolitan ecclesiastical institution. Rather, the missionaries were to make a hurried and world-wide declaration of the gospel in order that sinners might be without excuse for their lack of readiness to confront Christ on the Judgment Day.

Of the four evangelists, only "John" had ventured the suggestion that judgment had already been executed upon unbelievers when they refused to accept Christ (5: 24-29), and that his return was realized in the coming of the Comforter to support the disciples in their missionary labors (15: 26 f.). This was not, however, a widely prevalent opinion. In the main, preachers still advocated the Jewish ideal of an approaching cataclysm for which it was the peculiar task of Christian leaders to prepare people in the Gentile world. It was a daring hope that for many decades yet to come carried believers in Christ confidently through periods of sore affliction in their desperate conflicts with heathen enemies. But it was the shell rather than the kernel of the evangelistic message. Regardless of what the future might have in store for him, the immediate duty of the devout Christian was to preach throughout the Roman world and make disciples of all the Gentiles, receiving them into the membership of the church and teaching them to observe the commandments of Jesus (Matt. 28: 19).

CHAPTER III

EARLY BUILDERS OF A CHRISTIAN SOCIETY

The earliest advocates of Christianity were concerned primarily with winning converts. At the outset they scarcely realized the difficulties to be encountered in building up a strong social institution. If the movement they championed was to be effectively perpetuated it would need in time to develop a more substantial organization. Only thus could it safeguard its own integrity and resist successfully the corroding forces of an increasingly hostile social environment. Greater variety in personnel, the multiplication of congregations, and widening contacts with the world at large rapidly augmented the church's problems. The appointment of officials, the more exact definition of creeds, the regulation of ritual, the development of a defensive apologetic, the determination of proper conduct, and the establishment of numerous instruments for personal and group control demanded more studied attention. These were tasks calling for the services of a new generation of creative leaders.

Ignatius

From an early date an important Christian congregation had existed in Antioch, the chief city of Syria. Here, it is said, the advocates of the new religious movement first received the name "Christians" (Acts 11: 26). In the second decade of the second century, this church's leader, then called a "bishop," an "overseer" (*episkopos*), was a man named Ignatius. Indeed, he called himself "the bishop of Syria." We have no information about his earlier life and work. When he first emerges into the clear light of history he is a prisoner on his way to Rome where he expects to be thrown to the wild beasts in the amphitheater.

The journey from Syria to Rome was a leisurely one. According to the custom of the times the prisoner was in charge of soldier-guardians—Ignatius calls them ten "leopards"—who traveled sometimes by land and sometimes by sea, employing such means of conveyance as might be available. The route would lead first to Seleucia, the seaport of Antioch, then by water to Attalia on the south coast of Asia Minor. Thence by land the travelers proceeded through Laodicea, Hierapolis, Philadelphia and Sardis, to Smyrna, where they probably found a ship that carried them first to Troas and then to Neapolis in Macedonia. Beyond Philippi, the next stopping place, we know nothing about their journey. Undoubtedly Ignatius ultimately reached Rome, but what happened to him there is not recorded.

Ignatius seems to have feared that interference by the church at Rome might rob him of his coveted martyr's crown. In a letter dispatched to them while pursuing his tortuous journey, he pled with the Roman Christians not to put any hindrance in his way: "Let me be food for the wild beasts by which I shall be able to attain unto God. I am God's wheat and am ground by the teeth of the wild beasts in order that I may be found to be pure bread. . . . I would avail myself of the wild beasts prepared for me and I pray that I may find them eager. Indeed, I will entice them to devour me eagerly. . . . Let fire, cross and arrays of wild beasts, scatterings of bones, crunchings of limbs, grinding of the whole body, wicked chastisements of the devil, come upon me, only that I may attain unto Jesus Christ. . . . Permit me to be an imitator of the suffering of my God." Presumably Ignatius' yearning for martyrdom was fulfilled when at last he arrived in Rome.

On the journey, however, Ignatius enjoyed a considerable measure of freedom. Notwithstanding the agony he suffered from forced association with his bestial guardians, he was permitted to visit the Christian communities in towns through which he passed, and to receive deputations from neighboring churches. He might have viewed his trip through the province of Asia as a triumphal procession for the bishop of Syria. He was allowed to receive communications from his Christian friends and to write letters to individuals and churches. Seven of these documents have survived, and they reveal in an interesting manner the type and range of problems with which a zealous Christian leader of that day felt obliged to deal.

Local interference by the police authorities had now become a serious menace to Christian groups in various parts of the Empire. It was not until the middle of the next century that an imperial decree was promulgated demanding a general persecution of Christianity throughout the Roman world. In the meantime outbreaks of violence against the new religion were purely local affairs, but were none the less distressing for the churches involved. At Rome, Nero, on learning of the social unpopularity of Christians, used them as scapegoats to divert from himself the suspicion that he had set fire to Rome in 64 A.D. Under Domitian (81-96 A.D.), at Rome, and in the province of Asia especially, Christians suffered because of their unwillingness to accord divine honors to the emperor. Fresh outbreaks occurred again in the time of Ignatius. He does not say what the specific circumstances were that brought trouble to the church at Antioch, but we happen to know definitely what was going on at this time in Nicomedia, the capital of the province of Bithynia-Pontus.

When the new governor, Pliny the Younger, arrived in Bithynia-Pontus he found economic conditions at a low ebb in the province. He was told that Christians were chiefly responsible for the bad state of affairs. Their abstinence from all forms of idolatry had brought about the decay of the temples and the falling off of trade in such commodities as victims for the sacrifice, fodder for the animals, and products of the image-making industry. Enemies of the Christians became ready informers when they found an official with a sympathetic ear. Then, too, the government was almost hysterically suspicious of private assemblies, such as the Christians held at the homes of their members. Although Pliny admitted that he could discover nothing harmful done at these meetings, he had ordered them stopped. He had also arrested some Christians and demanded that they recant. He had made examples of some of the more recalcitrant ones by executing them, while others who were Roman citizens had been reserved for transport to Rome. On appealing to the emperor, Trajan, for instructions, Pliny was told that he had acted properly, but was advised in the future not to "seek out" Christians, and above all not to pay any attention to anonymous accusations. Apparently the acute outbreak of hostility soon subsided.

Probably Ignatius had been the victim of a similar outburst of violence in Antioch. Henceforth Christian leaders were to find themselves under the ever growing necessity of defending the existing Christian societies before the authorities of the state. But Ignatius did not turn his hand to this task. Apparently he was too ardent in his desire for the glory of martyrdom to feel any inclination to allay the hostility of the government. He left this task to his early successors. Then, too, on reaching Troas he learned that the storm at Antioch had passed and the church was once more enjoying peace. But there were other dangers within the congregations themselves that gave Ignatius much concern. These defects he sought earnestly to remedy.

One of Ignatius' gravest anxieties was the lack of adequate official guidance for the Christian congregations. The situation seemed to him to be getting out of hand. In the primitive type of democratic organization, the local church was governed by the older converts, the "presbyters," as they were called. These individuals were normally occupied with their personal affairs and thus could not devote full time to the needs of the new society. A younger man, free to give himself exclusively to this service, who would oversee the activities of all the small house-congregations within a city where the Christian membership was outgrowing its meeting places, was sorely needed. This functionary began to appear in some regions before the close of the first century. Ignatius, who vigorously urged the exercise of a more complete control by the "bishop," became one of the earliest and most outspoken champions of a rigid episcopal government for the Christian church.

Episcopacy was the means advocated by Ignatius for suppressing divergent opinions and practices that were now causing trouble in some of the Asian congregations. He would have the bishop supervise all the activities of the church, particularly baptism, public teaching, and the celebration of the Lord's Supper. Certain influential persons were advocating opinions that seemed to Ignatius especially pernicious. Since they held a characteristically Gentile view of the inherently evil character of matter, they believed that Christ had not clothed himself in real human flesh. His purity had been preserved by only seeming to be a true fleshly being, while in reality he had been a divine apparition. Hence they were called "Docetists," a name derived from the Greek word "to appear." But if Christ had not possessed real flesh and blood, then participation in the church's holy supper, and its belief in the physical resurrection of deceased believers, were vain. Ignatius was too devout an ecclesiastic to tolerate these aberrations. He denounced the new teachers in language that was always vigorous and sometimes vituperative.

Thus Ignatius contributed to Christianity a new emphasis upon both the significance of the episcopacy and the importance of sound doctrine. The bishop was to rule in the interest of unity within the local group and uniformity among all the congregations. Christianity would thereby become catholic, universal.. Ignatius is the first person, so far as we now know, to have employed the expression "Catholic" church. He said explicitly in his letter to the Smyrneans: "In matters pertaining to the church let no one do anything without the bishop. To be valid let the Eucharist be conducted by the bishop, or by one whom he shall approve. Wherever the bishop shall appear, there let the assembly of the people be, even as where Jesus Christ shall be, there is the Catholic church. It is not permitted without the bishop either to baptize or to conduct a love-feast; but whatever he shall approve, this also is well-pleasing to God, in order that all you do may be safe and valid."

BASILIDES, MARCION, AND OTHER GNOSTICS

A younger contemporary of Ignatius, Basilides of Alexandria, devoted himself with great vigor to providing Christianity with a more complete theological system. Culturally, Alexandria was the new Athens of the Roman world. Its university had now become famous, and under its shadow confused systems of speculation flourished. Here Christianity first became a literary propaganda, in any full sense of that term. Basilides and his followers were prolific writers. Although these pioneer literati of the new religion were destined to become anathema to the majority of their fellow-Christians, and were to bear the accursed name of heretics—the Gnostics—their work was exceedingly important for the development of Christendom. Without a knowledge of their activities, the labors of many orthodox churchmen in the second and third centuries will scarcely be intelligible.

Intellectual life in the Roman Empire was nourished largely by means of private schools conducted by individuals popularly known as "philosophers." The philosopher, having reflected upon problems of the day until he had reached definite conclusions, presented himself to the public as a teacher. He procured a room, or some other suitable place for meeting, to which he invited hearers and there expounded his views. As his fame spread, pupils came in larger numbers and from more distant parts. They remained until satisfied that they too had a message for their fellows, which they now proceeded to deliver on their own account. These philosophical lecturers, representing varied types of thought, were to be found all about the Mediterranean lands in early Christian times. As a matter of course, students paid the master fees, but the enterprise was not primarily a commercial venture. Its greatest compensations were of another sort.

Probably Basilides was not the first philosopher to include elements of Christianity within the scope of his thinking. Nor was he the first member of a Christian church to employ the philosopher's technique for advancing the cause of the new religion. Paul had already adopted this procedure in Ephesus when he hired a lecture room in the school of Tyrannus, where he discoursed at stated periods on the subject of Christianity. Christian missionaries, when expelled from the synagogues, were forced to adopt something of the contemporary philosopher's methods. But house-congregations, gathered at the homes of members where rites of worship took precedence over didactic activities, were more distinctive of early Christianity's operations. The formal Christian school, of the philosopher's type, did not clearly emerge until the second century, and the Gnostic teachers were its earliest sponsors.

Early in the second century Basilides, assisted by his son, Isidore, established at Alexandria a philosopher's school. They undertook a more doctrinaire elaboration of Christianity for their contemporaries. Throughout the second quarter of the century they carried on a vigorous activity employing both the spoken and the written word. Basilides is said to have composed a commentary of twenty-four books on his own version of gospel tradition, and to have written also many odes and hymns. Pupils were attracted to the school, some of them later becoming aggressive teachers who carried this educational propaganda far afield. A certain Valentinus migrated from Alexandria to Rome about the year 136, and taught there for over two decades.

He had distinguished colleagues and successors in the persons of Heracleon and Ptolemæus who flourished in the period between 145 and 180. In Egypt, Italy, southern Gaul and Syria these Gnostic Christian schools had become a conspicuous feature in the Christian situation by the close of the second century.

The more churchly minded Christian leaders deplored and sharply condemned the speculative novelties that Gnostic teachers introduced into Christianity. These new theologians were so individualistic, and so loosely bound to the traditional sanctions on which the life of the Christian society had been nourished, that their teaching seemed to menace its perpetuity.

Basilides and his disciples were much farther removed than earlier Christian leaders had been from the Jewish antecedents of Christianity. Before coming into contact with the new religion their interests and thinking had been shaped by a widespread Gentile yearning for escape from the evils of the world. The church had realized from the beginning that this world is an undesirable abode even for Christians, but its destruction was thought to be imminent. Although evils were mounting with the increase of persecution and the delay of deliverance, recent calamity could be viewed as evidence that the church was merely passing through the darkest hour before the dawn. But what had such a religion to offer to a suffering humanity that had not been reared upon Jewish expectations of deliverance by means of God's catastrophic intervention at a climactic moment in cosmic history? This question was all the more in point at a time when the social respectability of the Jewish people was at low-water mark in consequence of their revolutionary activities in Egypt, Cyrene and Cyprus, as well as in Palestine. They had been deprived of the right to set foot in their holy city, forbidden to practice circumcision, and forced to pay into the coffers of Jupiter Capitolinus at Rome the annual levy formerly contributed to their sacred shrine in Jerusalem.

Gnostic Christian teachers made a fresh attack upon the ever-present problem of evil and redemption. They approached it, not from Jewish postulates of thought, but from the presuppositions of a widely current type of Gentile speculation regarding the evil character of matter in contrast with the divine purity of an ideal immaterial world.

Basilides undertook to explain why holy martyrs, like innocent infants, were subjected to suffering. Ignatius might view the prospect of martyrdom as a mere incident or accident; his was not a philosophic mind that felt impelled to integrate every phase of experience into one all-inclusive scheme of thinking. Evidently Basilides was convinced that good and evil had to be placed in a logical relationship to one another. Good men ought not to be obliged to endure pain without an essential cause. Even if life was a mighty maze, it was not without a cosmic plan. Hence Basilides inferred that a good God would permit torture only when it served a redemptive purpose. It must be that the seemingly undeserved afflictions which overtook holy martyrs and infants were in reality a purging punishment either for hidden sins in the present life or for transgressions committed in an earlier stage of the soul's cycle of existence. Thus the universe was thought to be at its heart both good and moral.

When one undertook to fit the multifarious phenomena of the universe into one consistent scheme of thinking, the task invited an exercise of great imaginative skill. The

Gnostics devoted themselves with zest to this undertaking. The result was great diversity in many details of imagery employed by different Gnostic theologians, yet there was a fundamental unity running through all of their speculations. The goal of their common effort was the attainment of cosmic wisdom, a sublime knowledge—*gnosis* in the Greek language, whence they were called "Gnostics." Beyond the material world of sense they penetrated into the invisible world of supersensible reality—the world of ideal, inaccessible and pure Deity. This transcendental world was thought to be perfectly good, in contrast with the inherently evil character of the material world of physical sense. To release the soul of man from entanglement in the evil world of matter and guide it back to the transcendental world of the good God was, for the Gnostics, the supreme function of religion.

Gnostic theology was essentially an exposition of the doctrine of redemption. The feature of Christianity that most powerfully attracted the Gnostics was the figure of Jesus as redeemer. To him they yielded unquestioning allegiance, and they devoted themselves to the task of reinterpreting his redemptive work in accordance with their distinctive interests and ideas. He was a new emissary from the transcendental world of the good God who had descended into the evil material world in order to bring saving knowledge to the enthralled souls of men. Like the Docetists whom Ignatius abhorred, they were chary about linking Jesus too closely with a human body of real flesh and blood. The incarnate Word (*Logos*) of the Fourth Gospel and the preëxistent Christ of Paul were, for the Gnostics, the most valuable items in Christian tradition, in the light of which all else needed to be expounded.

The prominence of the Old Testament in the church also caused Gnostic theologians much trouble. It made the supreme God the creator of this inherently evil material world, an act unworthy of the absolute Deity of Gnostic faith. The divine being who had created the physical world and given the Law to the Hebrews must have been inferior to the absolute God. He was a lesser being, intermediate between perfect good and extreme evil. Adopting Plato's phrase, the Gnostics called him the Demiurge—as it were, a subordinate official who had, all unwittingly perhaps, mingled good and bad in his imperfect work. Accordingly, the current Christian habit of accepting the Hebrew Scriptures as a perfect revelation of Christ's redemptive program seemed to the Gnostics an incongruous procedure.

An interesting example of Gnostic interpretation of the Old Testament has survived in a letter written by Ptolemæus, a pupil of Valentinus. The interpreter credited one strain in the Hebrew Scriptures to God, a second part came from Moses only, and the rest was derived simply from the ancient Jewish people. But in the part that came from God there were three elements among which a distinction had to be drawn. First, there was the purely moral law, which had been fulfilled by Jesus. A second part, in which good and evil had mingled, had to do with punishments, like an eye for an eye and a tooth for a tooth. This had been done away with by Jesus. In the third division were the ceremonial laws regarding the Sabbath, circumcision, fasts, feasts, sacrifices, and the like. It was a mistake to take these literally; they should be spiritually interpreted. Thus the Old Testament was essentially a work of the Demiurge rather than a pure revelation from the absolute Deity. It was intermediate between perfect good and outright evil, and so had value for Christianity when properly understood.

One venturesome Christian, with Gnostic leanings, proposed to cut the Gordian knot by throwing the Old Testament bodily out of the church, and substituting in its place a strictly Christian collection of writings. This individual was Marcion. He was a practical business man, a shipowner from Sinope in Pontus, rather than a product of the philosophical Gnostic schools. About the year 140, his business brought him to Rome where he became an active member of the church. Tradition reports that he contributed approximately eight thousand dollars toward the funds of the church. But even this generous act could not save him from disfavor when he opposed the presbyters. The Roman church had always cherished fondly its Jewish heritage—too fondly even Paul had thought. And when Marcion accused the Roman Christians of violating Jesus' injunction against sewing new cloth upon an old garment and putting new wine into old wine-skins, the situation became critical. A community with strong Petrine leanings could not tolerate Marcion's radicalism.

Marcion withdrew from the fellowship of the Roman church probably about the year 144. He seems to have died by the year 160, but in the meantime he had founded a new Christian denomination with many adherents in various parts of the Roman Empire. These churches, which perpetuated their independent existence for centuries, were vigorously anti-Semitic. They rejected the Scriptures of the Jews, and declared the God of the Old Testament to be an inferior being who had created an evil world. Jesus, they said, had brought into the world for the first time the genuine revelation from the heretofore unknown but true

God.   They adopted as their scriptural guide the epistles of
Paul and the Gospel of Luke, as revised by Marcion.   Unlike the followers of Valentinus, they seem not to have been
chiefly interested in philosophical speculation but in the
organization and perpetuation of religious societies.   In
this respect they were a dangerous rival to the older Catholic churches.

On the other hand, Basilides' followers were educational-
ists rather than churchmen, philosophers rather than ecclesiastics.   They sought to promulgate a way of thinking,
without trying to organize a new denomination unless forced
by their opponents to hold separate assemblies for worship.
This policy made them all the more dangerous in the eyes
of their critics.   As a separated social group, a Marcionite
church quickly settled into a groove of its own along which
it moved side by side with the parent body.   But a more
individualistic propaganda, free to vary its form in accordance with the skill or inclination of its sponsors, like an in-
fectious disease whose germ has not yet been isolated, was
much more difficult to combat.   For this reason the churchly
minded Marcionites, although vigorously condemned, gave
orthodox leaders relatively less concern than did the exponents of the more speculative Gnostic schools.

By the middle of the second century the problems of
Christian leadership in the Catholic communities greatly
multiplied.   But the lines along which new constructive
work needed to be done had become more clearly apparent.
Increasing hostility from the authorities of the state demanded a stronger defense of Christianity's right to exist
as a recognized unit in the social order.   Its distinctive
status, alongside of Jewish religion to which it was closely
akin, needed more explicit elucidation.   This involved a

more thorough christianization of Old Testament teachings, a stricter canonization of specifically Christian Scripture, and a clearer exposition of the relation between the Christ of the church and the God of the Jews. And the conversion to Christianity of larger numbers of Gentiles interested in culture and philosophy called for greater literary and speculative activity than had previously engaged the attention of Christian leaders. The recognition of these necessities was in large measure a result of the contribution that Basilides, Marcion, and their followers had made to the growth of the Christian movement.

JUSTIN

The best-known Greek philosopher who first found himself comfortable within the Catholic church, and devoted his energies to defending its current traditions and practices, was Justin, now commonly called Justin Martyr. He was born of Gentile parents residing in the Samaritan city of Flavia Neapolis, the ancient Shechem and the modern Nablus. The exact date of his birth is unknown but by the middle of the second century he was an outstanding Christian apologist. He traveled from place to place like other philosophical teachers of the day, still wearing the philosopher's mantle but lecturing on the truth and reasonableness of Christian beliefs. On the occasion of his last visit to Rome he became involved in trouble with the authorities, and, with six companions, was executed by the prefect about the year 165.

Justin had spent his youth in quest of truth as taught by philosophers representing different contemporary schools. In one of his treatises, the *Dialogue with Trypho,* he describes the restless quest which issued ultimately in his acceptance of Christianity. At the outset he had spent some time in the school of a Stoic teacher, but finally left because he wished more definite knowledge than this school could give him about God. Then he attached himself to a Peripatetic, but early took offense at his master's concern for fees. Next he sought out a Pythagorean, who had a high reputation, but who insisted too much on preliminary studies in astronomy and geometry to suit Justin's tastes. He wanted to go straight into theology without passing an entrance examination in mathematics. Therefore, he attached himself to a prominent Platonist, probably in Ephesus. Here he found a measure of satisfaction.

Platonic concern with the transcendental world of immaterial ideas greatly appealed to Justin. He felt that he was on the way to true wisdom, the goal of which was a clear and convincing knowledge of God. While enjoying the quest, evidently Justin grew somewhat impatient at his delay in reaching the certainty that could bring his mind to rest. He yearned for a concrete and objective authority, a "thus saith God." While in this unsettled mental state he one day fell in with a stranger, a venerable old gentleman, whom he later discovered to be a Christian. This man told him about the Hebrew prophets whose wisdom had been given them through the inspiration of the divine spirit, and whose predictions had come to perfect fulfilment in Christ. Justin's imagination was kindled by this conversation. He was seized by a passionate desire to make the acquaintance of the prophets and their Christian interpreters. Here he found a philosophy, both speculative and practical, that satisfied his cravings for certainty and guidance. This was his conversion to Christianity. It may seem very unlike the conversion of Paul, but Justin was equally ready to die for his new faith.

One of Justin's outstanding services to the Christian cause was his defense of the church's right to exist unmolested in the Roman Empire. He wrote the first formal apology for the new religion, or at least the first one that has completely survived, and undoubtedly it was the most important literary defense that had been produced up to that time. It was in the form of an open letter addressed to the state authorities. The work seems to have been composed at Rome about the year 150.

Justin's logic is not very compelling, but his convictions are strong and are emphatically affirmed. Christians, he declares, are entitled to justice and a fair trial based on proved charges of criminality. It is not proper to persecute them merely for their name, coupled with a blanket accusation of atheism. He rather evades the point of chief importance to the authorities, or fails clearly to perceive it. When Christians refused to worship the official deities of the state they were, from the Roman point of view, menacing the safety of the government by slighting its divine protectors. When Justin alleged that the gods of polytheism were only evil demons, while Christians alone worshiped the truly divine powers, he spoke as a philosopher rather than a statesman. His reasoning was sound only on the assumption that his major premise—the invalidity of the state gods—was true. This the magistrates were, quite naturally, unprepared to grant.

It remained for later apologists to present more elaborately a new religious philosophy of state, by which Christianity's God was made worthy of reverence as the truly competent protector of the Roman Empire. Justin was not equal to this task; he came too early in history and his social vision was too limited. But he rendered the new religion a distinct service by insisting on the noble quality of Christian living. Christianity could with entire propriety advertise its morals; the Christian manner of daily conduct welcomed the full light of day. Justin craved from the authorities of the state an exact and impartial investigation into the character of the members of the church and into the activities of the new religious society.

The public could now read, for the first time, an account of what actually transpired at the private meetings of the worshiping Christian congregations and could make itself intelligently aware of the harmless character of the church's sacred rites. Popular suspicion that gross enormities were practiced at the meetings was without foundation. The actual performances were simple and dignified. There were two principal rites of the cult, initiation by baptism and the sacred meal called the Eucharist. Justin described each in some detail.

When new converts were to be received the entire membership joined with them in a preliminary period of prayer and fasting, after which they proceeded to a place where water was available and the initiates received the holy bath of regeneration. They thus attained to the "new birth" that Christ had prescribed as necessary for entrance into the Kingdom of Heaven. They were thereby released from the bondage to fate and ignorance that had previously enslaved them. Now they possessed freedom, knowledge, and forgiveness of sins. They experienced the truly divine "illumination." The congregation having reassembled for prayer, the new members were greeted with the holy kiss and the Eucharist was celebrated. An official whom Justin calls the "president of the brethren" took bread and wine mixed with water and, after appropriate prayers of thanksgiving, by the aid of "deacons" administered the elements to the communicants. The deacons also carried away a portion of the holy food and drink for those members who had been unable to attend the service.

Once a week meetings were held regularly on the day called Sunday. Both in city and country members gathered in one place. First they listened to reading from the "memoirs of the apostles" and from the writings of the prophets. Then the president of the congregation explained the meaning of the Scripture lessons and admonished his hearers to live in accordance with the teaching to which they had listened. The assembly stood during a period of prayer, after which the Eucharist was celebrated. After the rite had been observed, a collection was taken. The offering was purely voluntary. It was placed in the hands of the president, who used it to support orphans and widows, to help persons in distress on account of sickness or other misfortunes, to minister to persons in prison, and to aid needy strangers who had found their way to Rome.

Justin gave two reasons for the choice of this holy day among Christians. It was the day on which God, having dispelled the primeval darkness of chaos, had caused light to shine upon his created world; and it was on this same day of the week that Jesus had arisen from among the dead. He had been crucified on the day before that of Saturn and had arisen on the third day thereafter, on the Roman "day of the Sun." Hence the Christian Sunday commemorated not only the time of the world's creation, but it was also the birthday of Christianity and so supplanted the Jewish Sabbath.

There would seem to be no good reason why the Christian rites should have been viewed with suspicion, when other widely patronized cults within the Empire were observing closely similar ceremonies. Yet, by the same token, Christianity might appear to be an unnecessary novelty. Justin freely admitted the fact of similarity, but he wished to impress upon his public the supreme validity of the new religion. Others were mere imitations; it alone was genuinely authoritative. He would have everybody realize that while Christianity might seem to be a new religion, it was in reality the oldest of all. Moses had antedated all Greek teachers and poets, and such true wisdom as might have been embodied in Gentile philosophies and cults had been derived indirectly from the Hebrew lawgiver. Thieving demons, lurking about in Moses' vicinity, had snatched away stray morsels of God's revealed truth and had taught it to the Greeks in order to discredit by imitations the Christian rites and teachings when finally they should be authoritatively promulgated among Gentiles by preachers of the gospel. Certain elements of heathen philosophy and religion were true because in the last analysis they were really Christian.

How far Justin's argument from antiquity may have helped along the cause of the church among its opponents remains a question. But as an instrument for strengthening Gentile Christianity's confidence in itself, the apologetic thinking of Justin proved exceedingly valuable. By making the historic revelation given in the Old Testament, rather than human reason, the Christian philosopher's source of supreme authority, Justin set an example long to be followed by the learned men of the church. Incidentally, he also thereby cut the ground from under the various Gnostic teachers. In such of his writings as have survived he did not concern himself extensively with Gnostic activities, except to call Marcion and his brood minions of demons. But he gave himself assiduously to the closely related task of rescuing the ancient Scriptures from their Jewish possessors, while liberating Christianity from the stigma of a Jewish ancestry.

Christian theologians who followed Justin could build with assurance upon his defense of the new religion's full right to the divine revelation that had been given temporarily to the ancient Hebrews, whose descendants God himself had cast off in favor of Gentile believers in Christ. One could now believe that the Jews had quite misunderstood their own sacred book.

Justin paved the way for Christianity's solution of still another of its second-century difficulties. The church held dear the physical reality of the earthly Jesus, since it guaranteed the virtue of the Eucharist and strengthened confidence in a physical resurrection of believers. Gnostics, on the other hand, minimized the humanity of Jesus in the interests of a more assuredly divine Savior. The two extremes seemed inconsistent. Justin relieved the difficulty by subordinating logical consistency to the norm of divine revelation. The idea of a mediating divine agent, called the Logos (Word) by certain Greek philosophers, was laid hold upon by Justin to prove that Jesus had not brought an entirely new revelation into the world, as the Gnostics, and especially Marcion, had felt impelled to assume. On the contrary, Justin identified Jesus with the divine Logos who existed before the creation of the world and who had been employed as a mediator by God throughout the whole course of his dealings with the world. It was the Logos who had inspired Moses and the prophets in times of old. Sometimes he had appeared as fire, sometimes his manifestations had been incorporeal, but in Palestine at the beginning of the Christian Era he had become a real man. He had submitted to death, which the demons had induced the Jews to inflict upon him, but by his triumph over death he had broken forever the power of the demons.

Justin did much to strengthen the position of the Catholic church. Yet he was neither an outstanding ecclesiastical leader nor a great creative genius in systematizing Christian dogma. But he served well his day and generation. Posterity did him no injustice when it cherished his memory more lovingly as a saint and martyr than as a churchman and theologian. He was at his Christian best in the presence of the hostile Roman magistrate. In the course of his trial, the prefect said: "Give heed, you who are called a learned man and think you know true teachings, if you shall be beaten and beheaded do you believe that you are about to ascend to heaven?" Justin replied deliberately in the affirmative. Growing impatient, the prefect categorically demanded that Justin and his companions sacrifice to the gods: "Unless you obey you shall be mercilessly punished." To this order Justin again replied imperturbed: "Through prayer we have confidence that we shall be saved if punished for the sake of our Lord Jesus Christ, for this will become our salvation and confidence before the more terrible and world-embracing judgment of our Lord and Savior." To this sentiment the others also agreed: "Perform your will, for we are Christians and do not sacrifice to idols." Unflinchingly the prisoners received their sentence: "Let those who will not sacrifice to the gods and obey

the emperor's command be beaten and led away for de-
capitation in accordance with the laws."

Irenæus

Before the close of the second century Christianity had
established itself in southern Gaul. At the two principal
cities, Lyons and Vienne, in the valley of the Rhône, Christian congregations had been set upon by hostile mobs who
initiated a violent persecution in the year 177. In the outbreak the aged bishop, Pothinus, had died while in prison,
and the leadership of the Christian cause in that territory
fell to Irenæus, a prominent presbyter of the church at
Lyons. He now became the bishop. He was originally
from Asia Minor, where he had been born about the year
140. Other members of the churches in Gaul are known
to have been Asiatics, yet there were also many native converts in the congregations at Lyons and Vienne.

Irenæus had been for some time busily engaged in missionary labors. While Greek was the formal language of
the church in the cities of Gaul, as also in Rome, in his
daily work Irenæus was accustomed to use mainly the Celtic
tongue of the country. Had he written an account of his
practical activities as a presbyter and a bishop, undoubtedly
it would have been immensely interesting to us. But we
have not been thus favored. Details of his busy life are
now known only very imperfectly from incidental references to his career in later Christian literature, and by inference from two works of his own composition. In response to the request of a friend, who seems also to have
been a Christian teacher holding a responsible position,
Irenæus wrote, in five books, a treatise designed to unmask
and refute the Gnostics. Later he composed also a sum-

mary of true Christian teaching, a "manual of essentials," for the benefit of a friend called Marcianus. These writings were completed about the year 190, and perhaps their author was active for another decade. The exact date and circumstances of his death are not known.

Irenæus' contribution to the Christianity of his day was very great. He was not a philosopher, like Justin, but a practical churchman concerned primarily with the regulation and strengthening of the Christian society. He labored to maintain the orderly unity of Christendom, to defend its traditional heritages from Judaism and from its own apostolic forebears, and to safeguard its rites and doctrines against the vagaries of Gnostic speculations. He must have been fully aware of the menace of persecution, for the Christian communities at Lyons and Vienne had suffered severely from the violence of their enemies in 177 A.D. But in the books that have survived from his pen Irenæus has not dealt in particular with this phase of the Christian situation.

The spirit of the man is happily reflected in a fragment of his correspondence with Bishop Victor of Rome. A difference in the date of observing Easter had become acute. In Asia Minor the prevailing custom had been to commemorate the death of Jesus on Passover day in each year (the fourteenth day of the Jewish month Nisan), irrespective of the day of the week on which it might fall. In Rome a different practice prevailed. There the day of the week was made the focal point of the Easter celebration. Friday was observed as the day of the crucifixion and the resurrection was commemorated on the following Sunday. Thus Easter had always to be observed on a Sunday. As yet there was no legislation of the church on this subject, one practice being general in Asia and the other common in the West. In his youth Irenæus had conformed to the Asian custom, but in Gaul he seems to have followed the Roman.

Victor, the bishop at Rome (189-198 A.D.), became irritated by the appearance in his city of agitators for the Asian manner of observing Easter. Accordingly, he took vigorous action, not only against this irregularity in his own parish, but in all parts of Christendom. In a letter to Bishop Polycrates of Ephesus, at that time the leading church of Asia, Victor demanded the substitution of the Roman for the Asiatic practice, and apparently threatened to withdraw fellowship from all churches that refused to obey his order. Polycrates was not slow to reply that he followed the original observance of the church in Asia attested by the practice of all the great Christian lights of that region from the beginning down to his own day. He had been a Christian for sixty-five years, was familiar with the entire holy Scriptures, and did not propose to be frightened away from his sacred customs by the terrifying words of Victor. God rather than men was to be obeyed. But Victor, too, was stubborn and was about to lay a charge of heterodoxy against all churches that persisted in disagreeing with Rome.

At this point Irenæus took up his pen in the cause of peace. He conceded that the Roman practice was preferable, notwithstanding the antiquity of the Asian observance. But he sharply censured the pugnacious Victor, whose hasty action threatened the peace of Christendom and might have led to a serious cleavage in its ranks. Irenæus maintained that the essential thing was the common faith commemorated by the divergently observed rites. Ancient worthies of the church had recognized such minor differences, but had subordinated them to the higher ideal of Christian brotherhood. Love and peace ought not to be sacrificed on the altar of ritual regularity in all the details of church practice. It is true that Irenæus wished to have regularity, but not at too high a price. Brotherly unity was preferable to mechanical uniformity. And for the time being at least, his spirit seems to have prevailed.

Irenæus' dealings with the Gnostics were tempered by no such spirit of conciliation. In them he saw only a menace to the Christian society, a malady to be purged out by every means in the power of the church. He sought to expose the erroneous character of their views, he denounced their manner of life, and he laboriously expounded an interpretation of Christian faith and practice designed to fortify Catholic Christianity against their insidious propaganda. With prodigious patience he leads his readers through the dreary mazes of Gnostic speculation and leaves them at the end of the journey thoroughly weary and ready to concede from very exhaustion, if for no other reason, that the heretics are a worthless lot.

Moderns, who are likely to find Irenæus tiresome reading, may miss his real significance as a creative leader for the Christianity of his day. His service to the church at the close of the second century, in fortifying the society against the forces of disintegration, in establishing ways of thinking that fused mystical experience with reflective theology, and in confirming the validity of traditional inheritances, can hardly be exaggerated. Gnostic rejection of the Old Testament, and degradation of the Creator to the status of an inferior divinity; suspicions regarding the genuine humanity of the Christian Savior, with the implied inefficiency of baptism and the Eucharist; and skepticism as to the power of the church to save the entire man, both body and soul, or kindred heretical aberrations, were doomed for centuries to come after Irenæus had accomplished his work.

Irenæus may fairly be called the founder of the ancient Catholic church as an institutional establishment; or, perhaps better, the creative architect who fitted its parts together into an imposing whole, insuring a consistency and solidity such as had never before been realized. It now had a clearly formulated rule of faith, which in all essentials is the so-called Apostles' Creed. In addition to the Old Testament, successfully rescued from Gnostic skepticism and interpreted in conformity with the moral and revelatory necessities of Christianity, it now had also an authoritative four-fold gospel. It had also acquired an elaborate theological system, not founded on the speculations of individual Christian philosophers, but rooted in the life and ritual of the Christian society. And it had been given a fundamental principle of unity, with the Roman church as the apostolic source from which radiated to all parts of Christendom the divine will of its founder. While anyone who desired to perceive the truth would find the genuine apostolic tradition in every church throughout the world, its most prominent repository was the church of Rome, "founded by the two most illustrious apostles, Peter and Paul." Hence it was fitting that every orthodox church, and orthodoxy was to be found in every true church, should agree with Rome since it held the most distinguished position in Christendom.

CHAPTER IV

PROTAGONISTS OF A CHRISTIAN
CULTURE

During the second century Christianity made notable progress in establishing its institutional integrity throughout the Roman world. The movement, which at first had depended for its existence chiefly upon the effective activity of individual preachers with an appealing personal message, slowly solidified into a distinctive social unit. Under the guidance of able leaders it gradually built up for itself a substantial organization. It evolved a system of government by officials charged with the direction of its affairs. Deacons, presbyters and bishops, with a varying body of assistants, bore their respective responsibilities in the administration of the congregations' activities. Much attention was also given to securing uniformity of opinion and practice both among members of the same community and throughout Christendom at large. Thus a new religion, conscious of a definite mission and intent upon preserving its solidarity, was added to the welter of cults already current in Roman society.

The new religion was in the Roman Empire to stay, even though leading churchmen may not as yet have realized how important a part Christianity was to play in future history. The early Christian expectation of God's intervention to annihilate the contemporary culture slowly retired into the background of theological theory. This once vivid hope grew dim and quite disappeared with the passing of the years and the elevation of Christianity to a more stable position in society. It now became the task of the church to capture the present world and transform it into a Christian civilization. Temporary outbursts of local hostility, or even imperial decrees designed to wipe out the church in all parts of the Empire, could not divert Christianity from its course. It was destined to triumph over all foes, and to become in the fourth century the dominating religion of the Roman world.

In the meantime Christian leaders found themselves charged with many new and difficult tasks. They had to make a Christianity suited to endure by functioning effectively in the ancient world. In other words, they had to christianize Roman civilization—the industry, commerce and morals characteristic of its life; the educational, literary and artistic activities engaged in by cultured people; and even the administration of the government. Advocates of Christianity had to learn to act on a world-stage, and to play leading rôles. An emerging Christian culture, to displace and transform heathenism, called for able protagonists. And these appeared in due time. In the course of two centuries they elevated Christianity to a position of preeminence in the moral, economic, intellectual, political and religious life of the Roman Empire. Christianity became genuinely cosmopolitan in its outlook and Mediterranean culture became formally Christian in its allegiance.

Tertullian

Tertullian was born of heathen parents at Carthage in North Africa, perhaps about the year 160. His father was a Roman centurion, an important military official, serving under the governor of the province of "Proconsular Africa." Carthage was its principal city and, next to Rome, the most prosperous urban center in the West. Unlike Alexandria, where Hellenistic influence predominated, Carthage was distinctly a Latin city that had remained less affected than even Rome itself by contact with the East.

North Africa was one of the most prosperous areas in the Empire, and life at Carthage displayed in acute form all the strength and weaknesses of a characteristically Roman civilization. Wealth abounded side by side with extreme poverty. The upper classes were strong for education, and the city gave to the Empire some of its most distinguished rhetoricians and lawyers. Heathen immoralities also flourished. Theaters and gladiatorial games stimulated the thirst of the populace for coarse jests and bloody contests. It must have been one of the most forbidding spots on earth for the cultivation of Christian conduct and ideals.

No one now knows how Christianity first came to North Africa. But in the last quarter of the second century there were vigorous Christian communities at different places in this territory. Sometimes these congregations were violently hated by the heathen populace who took a savage delight in witnessing the misfortunes of Christians executed by the headsman or thrown to the wild beasts in the amphitheater. Yet the church drew into its membership some persons of great intellectual and spiritual distinction. One of the best known among them is Tertullian, who in middle life turned from heathenism to Christianity and for thirty odd years thereafter consecrated his unusual powers of mind and pen to the service of the Christian cause in Carthage.

Unfortunately Tertullian's extant writings contain no

description of the circumstances under which he was converted. He wrote no spiritual autobiography, as did his distinguished fellow-countryman, Augustine, two centuries later. But the warmth and ardor of the North African blood marked them both as restless spirits ever in search of higher attainments in piety. Even while counseling others to emulate the Christian virtue of patience, Tertullian felt impelled to say of himself: "Most miserable me, I am ever aflame with the fire of impatience." He pursued so intently his quest for moral rectitude, his yearning for inner emotional satisfaction, and his desire to restore to African Christendom the spiritual power of the primitive church, that he finally allied himself with the puritan sect of the Montanists and thereby lost the reward of elevation to sainthood in the later church. But no one was able to impugn his moral character or to question his sincerity. And his successors in the church fondly cherished his memory and profited extensively from his labors.

Tertullian's conversion tempts our imagination. Some unique event must have occurred to cause a man of his education and temperament to abandon a prosperous and distinguished legal career for the service of a popularly despised religious cult. He had received the finest type of Roman literary education which made him a master of the Latin tongue and competent even in the Greek language. From Carthage he had gone to Rome to complete his training and practice his profession. He had been, as the Romans said, a *causidicus*, a court attorney, and apparently an eminently successful one. Had it been on some occasion when a Christian was haled into the Roman court and summarily condemned to execution that Tertullian's attention had first been directed toward Christianity? Had his innate

sense of justice been aroused by the harsh procedure and
his admiration awakened by the noble fortitude of the persecuted religionists?   Perhaps, but this is pure conjecture.
Yet it is plausible.   What one does know is that among
the earliest and most vigorous of Tertullian's works—in
fact, among the finest examples of early Christian writing—
are his *Apology* for Christianity against its persecutors and
his letter *To the Martyrs*.   Both were written about 197,
soon after he had returned to Carthage where he attached
himself to the church.   When he remarked that "the blood
of the martyrs is the seed of the church," had he in mind
his own conversion experience?

It is commonly assumed that Tertullian, having abandoned his professional career, returned to Carthage around
the year 193.   Henceforth he lived as a private citizen,
evidently with ample personal income, devoting his energies
to the Christian religion.   Throughout his life he remained
a layman, serving perhaps as a teacher of candidates for
baptism—the *catechumens*—but always ready to defend
Christianity against enemies or heretics, to advise the brethren on moral and spiritual matters, to defend the rites and
teachings of the church, and to condemn the evils in contemporary heathen society.   Throughout his career he was
a puritan of the puritans, and this ideal he enforced with
all the power of his legal mind, fortified with a mastery of
speech that has rarely or never been equaled in the history
of the church.   He knew how to be tenderly persuasive, but
he rarely indulged this mood.   Severe and uncompromising
with himself, he demanded a similar course for everyone
else, and admonished friends and foes alike in language
that was frequently intolerant, sarcastic and cruel.

The full extent of Tertullian's contribution toward the

making of Christianity in North Africa at the dawn of the third century is hard to evaluate. But various features of his work stand out conspicuously. Perhaps the first place should be given to his moral propaganda, both in its criticism of the contemporary pagan culture and in its therapeutic significance for the Christian society. No previous Christian moralist had so mercilessly laid bare the monstrous evils of heathenism, and especially the heinousness of the government's treatment of Christians. The church was made more fully aware than ever before of the tremendous task to be accomplished in any attempt to take possession of Roman society. Yet Tertullian's readers could not fail to be heartened by his lively portrayal of the extent to which Christians had permeated every stratum of life in the Empire. He stressed also their loyalty to the state and its rulers, and the saving leaven their presence had injected into a troubled world. Contrary to popular belief among pagans, he affirmed that the ills of society had been much worse in pre-Christian times, while hope for relief lay only in the further growth of the new religion. It was able to save the Empire. In what seems to us almost a moment of weakness for Tertullian the rigorist, he declared that even Cæsars would have accepted Christ if God had not denied them this privilege.

If Tertullian stimulated Christian confidence in the triumphant invasion of Roman society by the church, his rigid prescriptions for the conduct of Christians in concrete relations with heathen neighbors must have seemed a serious impediment to success. Compromise was not in his Christian dictionary. When recounting facts, he recognized that members of the church were to be found in comparatively large numbers in all the principal occupations of the day.

Momentarily, he spoke boastfully of the new religion's success. But in almost the same breath he demanded that a Christian should choose starvation rather than earn a livelihood in a calling that required contact with idolatrous customs. He erected inviolable taboos against either social or business contacts with friendly heathen neighbors. Such were his ideals, but such was not current Christian practice.

Had all his brethren enjoyed the personal economic independence of Tertullian, the retired Roman advocate who may have inherited from his father a substantial family legacy, his strict admonitions against mingling with the world might have been practicable. But the great majority of Christians were not thus fortunately circumstanced. They were compelled to follow Paul's advice encouraging converts to continue in their former callings even after conversion. In fact, they were all too ready to follow this course. The church was in serious danger of becoming a worldly rather than a spiritual institution. This fact was keenly sensed by Tertullian, and although it would have been fatal to Christianity's prospects of success in the Roman world had the church adopted wholesale and in literalistic fashion the rigidly separatist ideal preached by him, a voice of protest against worldliness was sorely needed. The church did not become puritanical, but the legacy of his rigorism continued to be a healthful factor of great importance in the future history of Christianity.

In still other respects Tertullian contributed much to the new cause. His scathing condemnation of heretics and his refutation of Jewish critics gave added strength to the Christian apologetic. He was not a philosopher, in the current meaning of the term, and he scornfully protested against what seemed to him a vicious tendency to produce "a mottled Christianity" composed of Stoic, Platonic and Aristotelian elements. Yet he really did more than most of his contemporaries to capture for the church the essential strength of the intellectual and cultural life of the West. Through his influence prominent features of Stoicism, like the corporeality of the soul and its inherent goodness—it is "naturally Christian"—became a Christian possession. And, above all else, the magnificent heritage of Roman legal thought and terminology was captured by him for the church. He was, like many a modern theologian who claims for Christianity full title to the findings, language and imagery of present-day scientific thinking, a daring plunderer of the Egyptians.

Although Tertullian was not an ardent churchman, and in the later years of his life was a severe critic of his Catholic contemporaries, he was nevertheless a staunch defender of the Christian tradition. His nonconformity was in the realm of moral rigidity rather than in the sphere of ecclesiastical procedures or dogmas. He vigorously affirmed the validity of the sacred rites of baptism and the Eucharist, he contended for the true faith against heresies, and he stoutly supported the principle of central authority, even the authority of the Roman church.

CYPRIAN

There were numerous Christian congregations in North Africa by the middle of the third century. About the year 240, ninety bishops were available for a council that condemned as heretical the bishop of Lambesis. Evidently it was a period of lively activity, which had brought into prominence the authority and responsibilities of the bishops. But beyond a few of their names, we know almost nothing about them. For a generation or more after Tertullian the leaders of the churches in this region escape us. Then suddenly the curtain rises, especially upon the scene at Carthage, and the famous Cyprian holds our attention during an eventful decade in the history of western Christianity.

Cyprian seems to have been born at Carthage, about the year 210. He was a thoroughly educated Roman of the upper classes, a professor of rhetoric and probably a practicing lawyer. He had learned the orator's art in its finest form, as represented by Cicero, and was a master of its technique. Apparently he always resided in Carthage where, after the custom of the times, he had a wide circle of cultured friends in whose company he delighted. He won distinction in his profession, he owned a villa, and he was counted among the well-to-do citizens of that prosperous city. Then, of a sudden, he completely reversed his former mode of life. On Easter in the year 246 he was baptized into the membership of the church, and was elevated to the position of bishop early in the year 249.

The conversion of Cyprian is not quite so obscure as that of Tertullian. Cyprian refers briefly to the event in a charming little treatise commonly called *To Donatus*, one of the choicest pieces of early Christian literature. He did not share the almost morbid delight of an Augustine in exposing the nakedness of his soul in the hour of its catharsis, and hence we are not able to penetrate very deeply into the circumstances attending his conversion. But his language is suggestive.

To Donatus, the first writing composed by Cyprian after he had become a Christian, embodies all the grace and eloquence of the Roman orator's manner. He represents himself in his gardens with a Christian friend passing the time in learned conversation under the inspiration of the pleasant landscape and in reflection upon the deep things of life. He meditates upon the utter vanity of his former career. He had enjoyed the advantages of wealth and honors, had participated in the characteristic pleasures of the age, and probably had often spoken or written in praise of the heathen culture to which he was habituated. Then his attention had somehow been arrested by the Christian summons to a new birth. When first his interest had been awakened, the possibility of realizing so radical a change in his way of living had seemed to him impossible.

Describing his condition at that time, Cyprian writes: "I wandered like a blind man in the darkness of night, tossed at random on the sea of the world. I was adrift, ignorant of my course, a stranger to truth and light. With my habits fixed as they then were, what the divine goodness held out to me for my salvation seemed difficult and improbable of realization. How was it possible for a man to be born again to a new life by baptism in saving water, to be regenerated, to lay aside what he had been, and without changing his body to change his heart and mind?" So great a conversion seemed to him quite impossible. One could not violently and instantaneously throw off the body with which he had originally been born or the habits of living that had become fixed through long years of custom. He continues: "I was caught and held in the grip of a thousand errors of my past life, nor did I believe it possible to extricate myself therefrom—so enslaved was I to my clinging vices, so despairing of better things, so indulgent of my faults, accepting them as boon companions."

Then the impossible happened. Cyprian does not narrate the steps in the process, but he exults in the outcome.

He could think of it only as an operation of divine grace. Contributing agencies vaguely flit in and out of the picture. One of Cyprian's deacons, who wrote an account of the bishop's life after his martyrdom, narrates that a venerable Christian presbyter had been instrumental in turning Cyprian "from worldly error to the knowledge of the true God." Undoubtedly Cyprian had also been introduced to the literature of Christianity, which made so forceful an appeal to his mind and heart that it became his constant source of inspiration throughout his subsequent life. He hardly could have known Tertullian personally, but he had early become acquainted with his writings and thereafter studied them with a devotion second only to that with which he read the Holy Scriptures. Like other representatives of heathen culture who turned to Christianity in that age, Cyprian seems to have been moved by disgust for the superficialities and immoralities of contemporary society, and by a desire for an authoritative guide in moral and spiritual affairs such as the church with its sacred books and its divinely instituted rites was able to furnish.

The change in Cyprian's manner of living was thoroughgoing. He contemplated the result with grateful satisfaction. "The regenerating water washed away the stains of my former life. A light from on high poured itself into my heart, purified of its pollutions. The Spirit, descending from heaven, changed me into a new man by a second birth." So Cyprian testified. Uncertainties now vanished, his darkness was turned into light, all difficulties were resolved, sin's chains were broken, and "earth-born flesh, animated by the Holy Spirit, had now begun to be of God." Action kept step with conviction. Cyprian immediately sold "almost all" of his property and used the proceeds for the care of the needy. His moral standards and practices were completely revised, in accordance with his new profession. And he devoted his entire time and energies to the advancement of Christianity and service for the brethren.

There was ample opportunity for service. Cyprian had barely been inducted into the office of bishop at Carthage when the most severe persecution yet experienced by the church was launched. Now for the first time an emperor set out to obliterate Christianity from all of his domains. The church as an institution was to be wiped out completely. Everybody was required to sacrifice to the heathen gods and to secure from the authorities certificates attesting that the law had been obeyed. By refusing worship to the ancient deities, who were the traditional protectors of the state, Christians brought down upon themselves the charge of atheism. Their neglect of the gods was an insult to the divine guardians of Roman society and thus a serious menace to the government. The "atheists" must be made to sacrifice. Those who failed to comply with the emperor's edict within a specified time, were to be imprisoned, or banished to forced labor in the mines, or executed if they persisted in their disobedience. The storm broke with full force early in the year 250, North Africa being one of the territories to feel its greatest violence.

The attack was directed first against the bishops, on the assumption that the Christian movement would quickly disintegrate if its leaders were removed. They seemed particularly responsible for perverting the older religious loyalties of the populace. Cyprian met the emperor's challenge by flight, but continued for about a year to direct the church's activities from his hiding place. When the emperor's death brought a relaxation of the persecution, Cyprian returned to Carthage there to confront within the church itself an array of new problems that inevitably followed in the wake of the storm. The bishop's wisdom, skill and ecclesiastical statesmanship were to be severely taxed within the next half-dozen years. The generalship displayed during this period in directing and reorganizing the activities of the Christian enterprise has won for Cyprian a distinguished place among the leaders of the church.

Cyprian's flight from Carthage to escape arrest would certainly have disgraced him in the eyes of Ignatius. But the lapse of a century had altered many Christian attitudes. The lust for martyrdom had appreciably waned; the demonic persecutor was to be thwarted rather than welcomed. Cyprian could affirm with a clear conscience that his act had been motivated, not by personal fear, but by an altruistic impulse. In this way he could best defeat the malicious purposes of the emperor and render the most effective service to the Christian congregation. Some members of the church were still zealous for the glory of martyrdom, if not in the extreme form of actual execution, yet in the milder type of "bearing witness" by imprisonment or other nonfatal modes of suffering for the cause. These persons, like drafted soldiers returning uninjured from war, were not immune from the temptation to play the part of heroes. Individuals of this sort in the church at Carthage caused the bishop some embarrassment. But his greatest difficulties emanated from another source. Large numbers of Christians had obeyed the emperor's decree by participating more or less extensively in heathen rites, or by otherwise securing the required certificates. These were the "lapsed" members of the congregation who, when the persecution relaxed, sought to be restored to their former fellowship. They furnished Cyprian one of his most crucial problems.

To deal with the lapsed was only one aspect, though perhaps momentarily the most acute, of a larger task now confronting Christendom. If the church was to remain in the world, gathering unto itself adherents with varying aptitudes for piety and subject to ever widening contacts with heathen society, it must redefine its conception of what a church should be and formulate more elaborately its scheme of controls and disciplines. It was in this area of development that Cyprian made his greatest contribution toward the further expansion of the ecclesiastical organization. His heritages from the past as a man of affairs in Roman society stood him in good stead in this crisis.

The social solidarity of Christendom was as sacred to Cyprian as the unity of the Roman Empire was to the imperial ruler. In order to realize this ideal for Christianity, it was necessary to recognize the ultimate authority of an official control. This Cyprian found in the episcopacy. As in Roman political thinking sovereign authority (*imperium*) resided in the office rather than in the individuality of the emperor, so the episcopacy was for Cyprian an authority superior to, and more all-embracing than, the power of any individual bishop. Cyprian was still enough of an idealist to believe in the existence of a real Christian unity above and beyond any mechanical uniformity enforced by a centralized administrative machinery. Had his relations with the Roman government been more congenial he might have drawn the practical inference, as later Christians did when the state had legalized their religion, that ecclesiastical unity could be insured only as obedience was rendered to one bishop for all Christendom, just as political unity required the recognition of one emperor for the entire state. This step in thinking Cyprian did not take. He maintained the ideal indivisibility of episcopal authority, shared in alike by all true bishops. Hence discord among bishops, if they are genuine, is impossible; and there is no place for a "bishop of bishops."

Cyprian had no time to waste in spinning fine theories. He was by necessity, if not also by inclination, a man of action. His doctrine of episcopacy, often considered his most noteworthy contribution to the ancient church's institutional development, was formulated in response to an immediate practical demand. During the fourteen months of his absence from Carthage the face of the Christian world had, one might say, been radically altered. For the first time in history Christianity had been universally challenged by a prohibitory imperial decree. Two sovereign powers, the church and the Roman state, were now formally and openly pitted against one another. The emperor, representing the state, had aimed his persecution especially at the clergy, representing Christ. The chief imperial enemy had been suddenly removed by death but he was sure to have successors, and the church needed more than ever before the guidance of properly authenticated leaders, particularly bishops.

Cyprian remarked that persecution was not the only danger to be feared. Sadly enough, the church had emerged from its recent trials no longer a unit, but a divided society rent by internal conflicts. It might have been likened to a state in the throes of civil war. Central authority needed to be reëstablished by recognizing anew the sovereign power of the episcopacy as the one divine institution founded by Christ. During Cyprian's absence from

Carthage a deacon supported by five presbyters had set himself up in opposition to the bishop. Then, too, certain persons who had suffered imprisonment or other distresses for confessing Christ during the recent persecution, yielded to popular reverence for their fidelity and arrogantly assumed authority to forgive the lapsed and restore them to fellowship in the church without the permission of the more cautious Cyprian.

In Rome also there was a similar state of chaos. Its bishop had been killed early in the persecution, and for several months the office had remained vacant. When finally a successor was elected in the person of Cornelius, who represented the more moderate attitude in dealing with the lapsed, the rigorists elected as rival bishop a certain Novatian who refused any absolution to the lapsed. Moreover, there were two rivals to Cyprian, one standing for the extreme of laxity and the other for absolute rigidity. Thus there were three officials claiming episcopal authority in Carthage, and two in Rome. Plague and famine added to the distress. At a time when the church ought to have been consolidating its strength and resources in preparation for a possible renewal of hostility by the state and in ministering to the needy and afflicted, it was dissipating its energies in party strife and the pursuit of personal ends.

The great need of the hour was unity, which Cyprian felt could be attained only by the reassertion of episcopal power. His statesmanlike procedure was to assemble councils, made up of bishops of other dioceses in North Africa, and by this means he sought to secure concerted and authoritative action. It was at the first of these councils, convened in the year 251, that he presented his impassioned plea for the recognition of episcopal control as stated in his famous tract, *On the Unity of the Church.* The document is no mere rhetorical essay composed in the quietude of his gardens, nor is it the broodings of an ecclesiastical theorist. Rather, it is a page from the book of life, throbbing·with anxiety for the preservation of Christianity's integrity and inspired by faith in its divine origin and future triumph.

Tenderly but firmly, Cyprian condemns all dissidents. They are guilty of the vicious crime of rending the seamless robe of Christ. The Lord who is the fountainhead of truth had built his church on Peter and had commissioned him to "feed my sheep." While Christ had given equal power to all the apostles, endowing them with the Holy Spirit and authority to remit or retain men's sins, he named Peter specifically in order to indicate unity. He and the rest of the apostles shared equally in honor and power, he being designated first to demonstrate that the episcopal authority began in unity and must ever so remain. "This unity we ought to hold fast and justify, especially we bishops who preside over the church, in order that we may prove that the episcopate itself is one and undivisible. Let no man deceive the brethren with falsehood, let no man corrupt the truth of the faith by treacherous prevarication."

Cyprian was, of course, addressing an assembly of bishops. But certainly he was not playing to the gallery; he was thoroughly sincere. His claims were made, not on his own behalf, but for the welfare of the church. And he mercilessly followed his argument to its logical conclusion. Certain inferences were inevitable. Beyond the pale of an episcopally governed communion, there could be no salvation: "No one can have God for a father who has not the church for a mother." A dissenting community is without divine life. A branch torn from its stock buds no more; a rill cut off from the spring will dry up; a ray of light cannot be plucked off from the body of the sun. Thus Cyprian struggled nobly, and not without a measure of success, to restore unity by bringing the churches of North Africa under authoritative episcopal control.

Cyprian's ideal of a united Christendom directed by a harmonious body of episcopal leaders was a grand vision answering to an imperative need of the hour. But it involved two dangers. It yielded too readily to perversion by an aggressive bishop who might restrict the theory to his own see, as did powerful Roman bishops in later times; and it implied a measure of uniformity for all Christendom that could not be realized in an expanding world-church within which elements of diversity had to be given a place. Even in his own lifetime Cyprian was to experience personally some of his theory's defects.

In his monograph on the unity of the church, Cyprian had contended that baptism could be effective only when performed by true bishops, since they alone could insure the forgiveness of sins and communicate the Holy Spirit to the candidates. Valid sacraments were possible only when administered by a valid episcopacy. Therefore persons who had been baptized by heretical ministers must be rebaptized when seeking admission to an orthodox communion. This conclusion was a perfectly logical deduction from Cyprian's premises. But it was not in universal agreement with former customs, nor with much prevailing sentiment concerning the inherent efficacy of the sacramental rite, regardless of the character of its administrators. Cyprian's view dominated at Carthage and at influential centers in the East, but was never generally accepted at Rome. When Stephen became bishop there in 254 A.D. he openly attacked Cyprian, and a bitter controversy followed. Stephen, alleging that he was the genuine successor of Peter, boldly severed communion with Cyprian and the church at Carthage.

A fresh outbreak of persecution at the close of the year 256 diverted the attention of the church to other issues. Stephen was executed at Rome, and Cyprian directed his energies to preparing his flock for the approaching ordeal. He was himself arrested and brought before the proconsul on August 30, 257. On refusing to sacrifice, he was banished to Curubis, a desolate place some fifty miles distant from Carthage. A year later he was recalled but was held practically a prisoner on his estate at Carthage. On September 13 he was thrown into prison, and the next day was brought to trial. When condemned to die for his refusal to obey the proconsul, his only reply was, "Thanks be to God." His execution followed immediately. Thus ended the stormy decade of his episcopal administration.

The debt of the church to Cyprian was indeed a vast one. He has quite properly been enshrined among its most revered saints. The Shakespearean dictum, that the good men do is often interred with their bones, does not hold true of him. His frailties were soon forgotten, while his virtues were generously applauded. His devotion to charitable enterprises, his diligence in moral discipline, and his valiant advocacy of Christian unity won him enduring admiration. Augustine's encomium is typical: "Praise be to him who made this man what he was, to set before his church the greatness of the evils with which charity was to do battle, and the greatness of the goodness over which charity was to have precedence, and the worthlessness of the charity of any Christian who would not keep the unity of Christ."

CLEMENT OF ALEXANDRIA

While Tertullian and Cyprian were bravely contending for a Christianity worthy of cultured people's respect in Carthage, a similar struggle was going on in the East, particularly at Alexandria in Egypt. The movement toward giving Christianity intellectual respectability had been initiated in Alexandria by Gnostic teachers, but the church generally had rejected their efforts and cast them out of its communion. The reasons for this exclusion have already become apparent. Yet Christianity had to come to terms with the current trend toward philosophical speculation if it were to become culturally respectable in the eastern part of the Roman Empire. The accomplishment of this task fell to the lot of the Alexandrian Christians. Intellectualism had to be rescued from degradation by the Gnostic heretics and made a legitimate possession of the church. Clement of Alexandria, thanks to his surviving writings, enjoys the distinction of having been the first effective toiler known to us in this enterprise.

As is the case with many other early Christian leaders, accurate biographical information about Clement is exceedingly meager. He must have been born about the year 150, possibly at Athens. Apparently his ancestry was heathen, for he seems to have been initiated in some of the mystery cults whose rites were familiar to him. His early education is known only by inference. But evidently he had been an eager student of Greek philosophy, for which he retained an ardent admiration throughout his life.

He believed that philosophy had been given to the Greeks, as the Law had been given to the Jews, to prepare them to receive Christ. Clement had absorbed substantial elements of both Platonism and Stoicism, and used them extensively in his interpretation of Christianity. He also had a wide familiarity with Greek authors, whom he often cited with approval. But he deliberately spurned the ornate style cultivated by the Greek sophists of his day. Truth, he thought, is more important than fine phrases; literary style is only the garment, which is of less account than the body. Had he given a little more attention to good literary form he might have made a stronger appeal to his contemporaries as well as to his modern readers. He seems to have labored under the delusion that the book of a theologian ought to be dull. In this respect he stands in sharp contrast to his Carthaginian contemporary, Tertullian.

Clement's education had been completed under Christian teachers. He records this fact himself, but says nothing about his conversion to Christianity. It may have taken place in a manner similar to that of Justin's. Following the custom of the time, Clement in his youth had sought out various teachers of whose fame he had heard. These he says were all "truly blessed and memorable men" who passed on to their pupils genuine apostolic traditions. One of these teachers he met in Greece; others were found in southern Italy, Syria and Palestine; but not until he came to Egypt did he discover the one who gave him enduring satisfaction. This master was Pantænus, the head of the Christian school in Alexandria.

Henceforth Clement made Alexandria his home. He became a presbyter in the church, but his chief work was in the school, of which he became head after the death of

Pantænus, perhaps about the year 190. He continued teaching and writing until persecution broke out in the year 202. Then he left Alexandria, in obedience to the gospel injunction that the persecuted in one city should flee to another. The scenes of his further activity are quite unknown, but his death is believed to have occurred about 215 A.D.

The personality of Clement and his contribution to the Christianity of his day are fairly evident from his books. He was a teacher and scholar dominated by a strong moral purpose and firm in his loyalty to the Christian faith. He valued highly the fellowship of the church, the cleansing and illuminating sacrament of baptism, the spiritual refreshment unto salvation derived from participation in the Eucharist, the sustaining power of prayer, the truth handed down in apostolic tradition, and the divine revelation contained in the ancient Scriptures. Yet his emphasis was intellectual rather than ecclesiastical; he was a scholar rather than a churchman. Without the least thought of disparaging the simple faith of the unschooled believer, he would have Christians rise to a higher state of virtue by means of true knowledge. On the foundation of faith one built a superstructure of wisdom in the truth derived from study of Scripture and the exercise of God-given reason. Thus without falling into the snares of the Gnostic heretics, the intellectual man in the church pursued divine wisdom and became the true "knower," the genuine "gnostic," to use a favorite term with Clement.

Religion and education were no longer antagonistic interests within Christianity for pupils trained in Clement's school. To establish this principle in Alexandria before the year 200 was a tremendous gain for the Christian cause in that environment. The same principle has had to be reaffirmed time and again under changing conditions in religion and knowledge all through the centuries down even to the present moment. But Clement developed still another important insight. He would revere the rational faculty implanted in man by God, but he would eliminate all arrogance and pride. Religious knowledge could not be acquired and maintained without the exercise of love. It was this virtue that most surely united the true gnostic to the Deity, cemented the brethren together in the church, and carried the Christian to victory in his contacts with the world.

Young men, trained for service under Clement's instruction, must have constituted a valuable asset to the Christian church. They were given a new vision of the use to which they could turn their intellectual powers, and were dis-·ciplined in the noble virtues of the Christian life. He lectured to them on the evils of polytheism in their environment. In his *Exhortation to the Greeks* he provided them with a text book that must have been exceedingly useful in their apologetic for Christianity when in controversy with their intellectually disposed heathen acquaintances. His treatise entitled the *Pedagogue*, or *Tutor*, was an invaluable guide-book for the direction of the religious life and the cultivation of Christian morals. It gave, in almost tedious detail, minute instructions for one's conduct. And, in a more philosophical vein, in still other lectures he showed how Scripture could be made to justify every conviction of the rational being by one who understood how to detect the spiritual meaning that remained veiled behind the letter of the text as read by the uneducated man.

No one who knew Clement needed to feel that Christianity was out of place in the present world. It was essentially a good world, for it had been created by a benevolent Deity, but it must be cleansed of the evils injected into it by men themselves. Even prosperity was God's gift, in spite of the fact that wicked persons had wasted their goods by indulging in immoral and prodigal luxuries. A Christian did not need to be severed from his property in order to be saved, but his soul must be purged of its selfishness and lusts. Also the highest intellectual attainments were entirely compatible with virtuous conduct, if the philosopher made God and divine knowledge the ultimate goal of his quest. Under this type of leadership the new religion was no enemy to prosperity and culture, but was the saving power by which these estimable endowments of God were to be turned to their proper uses.

ORIGEN

Alexandria produced still another conspicuous intellectual light in the person of Origen. He was the first Christian scholar who had been born and reared in a cultured Christian home. In the absence of dependable records concerning his youth, tradition toyed freely with his fame; he was called "a great man from infancy." However that may be, he was undoubtedly an unusual boy who early experienced sore adversity but remained firm in his determination to acquire learning and pursue the Christian way of life.

While Origen was in his seventeenth year his father, Leonides, was arrested in a persecution that was raging at Alexandria in the year 202. The son was so zealous for the faith that he would have rushed out to join his father had not his mother hidden his clothes to keep him at home. Origen had to content himself with writing a note to his father imploring him to remain steadfast. And Leonides did. He was put to death, the property of the family was confiscated by the state, and the mother with her seven children was left penniless. The father, a prominent and prosperous member of the church, is commonly assumed to have been a professor of Greek literature. At any rate he was a cultured man who had given much care to the education of his son. Probably the youth had also attended the lectures of Clement who was driven from Alexandria by this same persecution.

After his father's death Origen was befriended by a wealthy Christian lady who gave him shelter in her home, but he was unhappy because of the Gnostic leanings of the lady and another of her wards whose views were so unorthodox that Origen could not bring himself to join with them in the family prayers. He preferred true theology to free bed and board. At the same time he had set himself up as a teacher, for which task he had been prepared by his father's care. By selling his library, presumably his collection of Greek classics, he was able to supplement his income sufficiently to maintain a meager existence without further aid from his Gnostic patroness. He taught during the day and studied by night, thus perfecting himself in his chosen calling. At the same time he was active in Christian service to persons who still suffered from the persecution. His piety, learning, and skill as a teacher won him respect, and he was able to revive the Christian school that had attained fame under the leadership of Clement.

Origen was noted for his evangelistic zeal. Such of his pupils as were already Christians were trained to become more effective and intelligent members of the church. Those who were inclined toward Gnosticism, or who were still heathen, were persuaded to correct the error of their ways. Fees were accepted from pupils, but apparently on a purely voluntary basis. Origen declared it unscriptural to charge tuition. Jesus had driven from the temple those who sold doves, and since the dove symbolized the Holy Spirit which was the source of the Christian teacher's wisdom, Origen felt obligated to teach without pay lest by selling the Holy Spirit he be cast out of the temple of God. But the crumbs that fell from God's table were not forbidden. The laborer was worthy of his hire, yet the gospel was not to be preached for material gain. The Christian school was dominated by the missionary spirit. Its teachers were engaged in an altruistic endeavor to rescue for the church the intellectual life of the Roman Empire.

Intellectualism was not to supplant faith or to be a substitute for genuine piety. Origen insisted that the elementary faith of the Christian was far better than the abundant wisdom of the world, while the unadorned simplicity of Scriptural teaching was preferable to the seductive rhetoric of the most skilful heathen orator. The divine truth of the revealed Christian message was its supreme credential. Yet Origen held, as did Clement, that education was absolutely essential to the highest type of Christianity. Faith and knowledge were sharply distinguished, but they were not allowed to antagonize one another. Belief came first. One accepted a specific body of tradition and dogma sponsored by the church and possessed in common by the members representing every shade of intelligence. This simple faith was sufficient to insure salvation, but it was only the first step in Christianity. Further progress toward perfection required knowledge that could be acquired only by strenuous intellectual effort.

Origen chose this educational task for his life-work. Less generous than Clement had been toward the inspiration of Greek philosophers and poets, Origen restricted the sources of revealed wisdom more rigidly to the Scriptures and the tradition of the church. But he far excelled Clement in the effort to show that Christian truth, when properly analyzed and synthesized, covered the entire range of the best educated man's intellectual quests. Accordingly, Origen trained his pupils in logic and dialectics as aids to correct thinking and accurate expression. Geometry and astronomy were included in his school's curriculum, since these disciplines were fundamental to a clear understanding of the physical world and contributed toward the broadening and strengthening of one's mental grasp. The metaphysical theories of various philosophical schools, excepting only those of the atheistic Epicureans, were also carefully examined. These preliminary studies cleared the ground and prepared the student for Christian education's crowning work. This was the exposition and defense of Christian ethics and doctrine.

Origen is said to have written six thousand books! This statement sounds highly idealistic. Yet it is true that he was a prodigious worker throughout a professional career extending roughly over half a century. The first decade of his activity in Alexandria seems to have been a period of foundation-laying for the young scholar, whose reputation for religious sincerity and effective teaching rapidly increased. The number of his pupils gradually multiplied, some of the most distinguished being converts from the rival school of the Gnostics. Among them was a certain Heraclas, who later became an assistant teacher to Origen and still later rose to the dignity of bishop of Alexandria.

About the year 212, Origen paid a visit to the Roman church, evidently in the hope of gathering further inspiration for his work from that ancient seat of the faith. But he soon returned to Alexandria quite disgusted with the laxity he found current in the Roman community. He now handed over to Heraclas the more elementary instruction of the catechumens and concentrated his own attention on the study and exposition of the Scriptures. To prepare himself better for this task he now took up the study of Hebrew. Also he won over from the Valentinian Gnostic heresy a certain Ambrose, a man of means who was to play an important part in Origen's further work.

Origen's fame early spread beyond Alexandria. Shortly after his return from Rome, Demetrius, the bishop of Alexandria, sent him on a mission to Arabia at the request of the Roman prefect in Petra. The visit was a brief one, and Origen was back in Egypt when a popular uprising in the year 215 temporarily closed his school. He took refuge in Cæsarea, along with his friend Ambrose. His fame had preceded him, and at the request of the bishops of Cæsarea and Jerusalem he preached and expounded the Scripture to the Cæsarean church. This act was an ecclesiastical impropriety, from the point of Origen's own bishop, Demetrius, who had never ordained this brilliant professor. He was still a layman, and ought not to preach in the church. The local hostility in Alexandria having ceased, Demetrius recalled Origen who now resumed his former professorial and literary activities. He seems to have been back at his academic task by the close of the year 216.

For the next fourteen years Origen labored indefatigably at his teaching and writing. His friend Ambrose conceived an ambitious plan for bringing Origen before the

public. He was provided with a corps of shorthand writers
—seven, we are told—who worked in relays taking dictation, while a similar number transcribed the copy in long-
hand. The manuscript was then reproduced for the market
by professional copyists. Ambrose also suggested suitable
themes for prospective books, perhaps feeling that his finger
was more sensitive than the professor's to the pulse of the
reading public. Thus the first Christian "University Press"
began operations, with an aggressive business manager and
a cloistered scholar collaborating to make the enterprise a
success. The scheme may sound very modern, but it was
actually in vogue more than seventeen centuries ago, and it
is not easy to calculate its full significance for Christianity's
growing cultural prestige in the Roman Empire.

All went well until about the year 230, when Origen was
sent on a mission to Greece. He took advantage of his stay
in Athens to pursue some researches. But in passing
through Cæsarea, where he had many friends, he committed what turned out to be a grave ecclesiastical blunder.
The people wanted to hear him preach, as he had done on
his former visit. But he could not comply with this request
without offending Demetrius, for Origen was still unor-
dained. So the church authorities at Cæsarea proceeded
with his ordination. This action further incensed Demetrius, who looked upon it as an infringement on his prerogatives. Therefore he convened a synod first to banish Origen
from Alexandria and later to declare his ordination void.
Thereafter Origen took up permanent residence at Cæsarea,
where he taught and wrote for the rest of his life, adding
now regular preaching to his former duties. His work was
somewhat interrupted by a local persecution in 235, and
much more seriously by the general persecution of the year

250 that wrought so much havoc at Carthage and Rome. Origen was arrested and severely tortured, although he was released after the death of the emperor in the year 251. But the great teacher's health was badly broken by his sufferings and he died soon afterwards, probably in the year 254.

Origen was one of the most praised, and one of the most blamed, leaders in ancient Christianity. The vigor and independence of his thinking so offended some of his successors that he, like Tertullian, failed to attain to the dignity of a saint. But a dispassionate appraisal of his work necessarily accords him a preëminent place among the early champions of Christian culture. In this sphere his contribution to the church was outstanding. His study and interpretation of Scripture gave the Bible an unassailable supremacy in the literary life of antiquity. His treatise *Against Celsus* was not only the most effective apology for Christianity against its learned heathen critics, but it broke the force of that opposition for all future time. And his *First Principles*, though not a complete "systematic theology" in the modern sense of the term, was the most elaborate and thoroughgoing exposition of the total body of Christian thinking to be produced before the days of Augustine. For originality, creative genius, and mental grasp, he had no superior and few equals in the early Christian era, either within or without the church.

LACTANTIUS

The last forty years of the third century were kind to Christianity. During this period emperors were either friendly or indifferent; they did not light anew the fires of persecution. In the meantime the membership of the church rapidly increased and people of high station joined it in larger and larger numbers. Yet its triumph in the political sphere was far from certain. Its relations with the government were in a state of suspense, with the balances loaded rather heavily on the side of suspicion. The ancient gods of the heathen were still the legitimate protectors of the state. Until they could be dethroned and the administrative mind of the Empire induced to trust in the protection of the Christian's deity, a fresh outburst of persecution was always possible. This possibility became a terrible reality in the year 303. Suddenly the emperor Diocletian launched the bloodiest of all the attacks upon the church. It raged intermittently for a decade.

The Diocletian persecution produced another vigorous defender of Christianity in the person of Lactantius. He was neither an ecclesiastic nor a professional theologian, but was a cultured member of the laity. Probably several such persons, occupying important positions in society, even in the government, had gone over to Christianity in the forty-year period of the church's peaceful growth. The adoption of the new religion need not have occasioned special comment. The converts still went about their regular business and, after the custom of the day, pursued their religious inclinations according to their personal and private tastes, much as one does in modern society. This, apparently, had been true of Lactantius, who was the most prominent teacher of Latin oratory at Nicomedia in Bithynia, where the emperor resided. In fact, Diocletian had called Lactantius from North Africa a few years before to fill this important position.

Little is known of the earlier career of Lactantius. Presumably he had been born about the year 250, a native of

North Africa, where he had received the literary education for which that land was famous. In this respect he was a true successor of Tertullian and Cyprian, and a predecessor of Augustine. His adoption of Christianity seems to have occurred around the year 300, soon after his arrival in Nicomedia. But the events that led up to his conversion, and the character of his personal experiences in connection therewith, are not disclosed by any records at present available. It is apparent from his writings that ecclesiastically and theologically he was sadly deficient if judged by the standards of a Cyprian or an Origen or by the norms in vogue among later orthodox churchmen. Their favorite concerns were not his chief interests, and for this reason subsequent generations found it convenient to neglect or disparage his significance. But his moral integrity and Christian loyalty are beyond reproach, and his efforts to meet his cultured pagan contemporaries on their own ground certainly deserve serious consideration. He was genuinely Christian in his own way, although it was not the way of the more ardent—perhaps one might sometimes say the more bigoted—churchmen.

In Nicomedia, where the environment was overwhelmingly Greek, a professor of Latin rhetoric could hardly expect to enjoy the success that might have been his had he remained in Carthage or Rome. The East was not zealous to acquire Ciceronian skill in the use of the Latin tongue. Although Lactantius at first had the advantage of imperial patronage, it is not likely that students flocked in large numbers to his lectures. Generous fees were not forthcoming. With the outbreak of the persecution, imperial favor also ceased. But since hostility was directed chiefly against the church as an institution and its clergy in particular, Lactantius seems to have been able to continue his lectures. He suffered, however, from a "penury of pupils" and devoted himself to writing. In the year 305, as persecution became more oppressive, he withdrew from Nicomedia to parts unknown, but he kept on with his literary work in defense of the Christian cause. He may have returned to the city in 311 A.D. after Galerius, then the eastern emperor, issued his edict tolerating Christianity. Finally fortune proved more generous. Shortly after the year 313, when Constantine and Licinius as joint rulers of the whole Empire made Christianity legal throughout their domains, Lactantius was called to Trier (Treves), the imperial residence in the West, to become tutor to Constantine's son Crispus, then six or seven years of age. At that time Lactantius is said to have been a "very old man." We know neither the date of his death nor the events connected with the closing years of his life.

Among the products of Lactantius' pen, his treatise in seven books, called *Divine Institutes*, is the most important for an understanding of his contribution to the making of Christianity at the beginning of the fourth century. This work was produced during the strenuous decade of 303 to 313. The author was in a peculiarly favorable position to appreciate the feelings and attitudes of a large class of cultured persons whose antagonism to Christianity could not be dislodged even by an edict of imperial toleration. They were the aristocratic intelligentsia of Roman society, whose temper was political and practical rather than speculative in the Greek sense of the word. They ridiculed what seemed to them Christian naïveté in believing that a Divine Providence controlled human affairs, while Christians fanatically reviled ancient customs and flouted the power of the

state. The Christian philosophy of history and government
needed a new apologist who could approach the aristocrats
on their own ground and speak their language. The tirades
of a Tertullian, or the speculative reasoning of an Origen,
left these objectors cold. And the customary appeal of the
Christian apologist to the authority of the Scriptures had
no weight with them. Such arguments were thought unworthy of their attention.

Lactantius attacked Christianity's opponents on a new
front. Clement and Origen had despised, or had not cared
to cultivate, a fine literary style. That seemed beneath a
Christian's dignity. Lactantius took a very different view
of the situation. He would employ every device of the
rhetorician's art to win a hearing for his religion. His
ecclesiastical contemporaries might think him woefully ignorant of the Scriptures, but his antagonists were equally
ignorant, and were content so to remain. Perhaps he
realized the futility of fulminating against them with biblical phrases. Moreover, he had never really learned to
use these weapons. But he had mastered another technique, with which his audience also was thoroughly familiar.
He would adorn his apologetic address with every stylistic
charm at his command and present the scheme of Christian teaching as a jurist's philosophy of life phrased in the
imagery of an overruling Divine Providence. He chose the
very title of his work with this end in view. Christian
doctrine was put forth as a body of "Divine Institutes"
(*institutiones divinæ*) paralleling the familiar Roman notion of "Institutes of Civil Law" (*institutiones juri civilis*).
The point was extremely pertinent to the situation.

In all probability Constantine was familiar with Lactantius' work, and was measurably sympathetic with his

attitude toward the religious issues of the day.   One would like to know how far Lactantius had been influential in persuading Constantine to trust his political prosperity to the keeping of the "Divine Providence" to whom he declares his allegiance, and from whom he hopes to draw further help as a result of Christians' prayers.   His desire for this assistance is emphatically enunciated in his famous charter of toleration for the church.   Whatever may have been Lactantius' influence in bringing about this change in the attitude of the emperors, his apology was a much needed contribution toward the new religion's defense in the aristocratic circles of an effete Roman culture.

CHAPTER V

ARCHITECTS OF AN IMPERIAL CHURCH

During three centuries of growth Christianity had gradually drawn into its fold representatives of many interests and activities characteristic of Roman society. The final conquest was to be accomplished in the realm of politics, when imperial rulers would definitely align themselves on the side of the church and make their distinctive contributions towards the further development of the Christian movement. This new triumph was presently to be realized under Constantine and his successors.

CONSTANTINE

Constantine enjoys immortal fame as the first "Christian" emperor. But legends cluster so thick about his person and render his real character so obscure, that there is wide diversity of opinion today regarding the measure of his right to the Christian name. Moreover, his political and religious concerns were so closely entwined that they can no longer be clearly disentangled. One fact, however, is self-evident; Constantine's reign had immense significance for the history of Christianity. Whether we grant that he acted from sincerely religious motives, or suspect him of playing the part of a worldly-wise and scheming politician, we must concede that his was the master hand to transform Christianity, for better or for worse, into an imperial state religion. He was the royal patron who for a quarter of a century bestowed increasing favors upon the church. He was aggressively active in shaping the course of its development, and he bequeathed to his successors a policy of toleration and support that was never to lapse except for three brief years under Julian, the so-called Apostate.

Constantine's service to the church was inseparably bound up with the contemporary political situation. Diocletian, who became emperor in 284 A.D., has proceeded to reorganize the government on a new plan by which four administrators held office. There were two associate emperors called "Augusti," one being Diocletian with his capital at Nicomedia in Bithynia and the other, Maximian, stationed at Milan in northern Italy. Each emperor chose a "Cæsar" as assistant, who was to advance to the imperial dignity on the death or retirement of his superior. Diocletian's Cæsar was Galerius who resided at Sirmium in Pannonia, while Maximian's subordinate was Constantius who ruled the West from his capital at Trier in Gaul. Thus at its most strategic points the Empire had efficient leaders, all four working together harmoniously and effectively for the preservation of order within the realm and for the protection of the frontiers. It was a beautiful piece of administrative machinery driven by a four-cylinder motor that ran smoothly while Diocletian remained at the wheel. But when he voluntarily retired in the year 305, and persuaded his reluctant colleague Maximian to follow suit, the new machine quickly stalled. Once more the Roman world resorted to the destructive expedient of a civil war to determine the imperial succession. This situation furnished Constantine his opportunity.

When Diocletian retired, Constantine was a vigorous and resourceful young man in his early thirties. He was the son of the Cæsar Constantius by his first wife Helena, who is said to have been the daughter of a Nicomedian inn-keeper and a devotee of Christianity. When Constantius became a Cæsar he was required to put her aside and marry Theodora, the daughter of his Augustus, Maximian. Constantine had been kept at the court in Nicomedia as a pledge of his father's loyalty, but had there enjoyed full princely privileges. Undoubtedly he had become at least super-ficially acquainted with Christianity, perhaps largely under the influence of Lactantius to whom he later intrusted the education of the son who had been born to him by his mistress Minervina. . When Galerius succeeded Diocletian at Nicomedia, Constantine returned to his father in Gaul.

Constantine had been with Constantius barely a year, spent at York in Britain, before the latter died on July 26, 306. Forthwith, the army elected Constantine to succeed his father, notwithstanding the fact that the Diocletian pro-gram, now dictated by Galerius, provided for the automatic succession of a certain Severus, who had been made Constantius' Cæsar, to the vacant office of Augustus. Similarly in Italy, the ambitious son of the retired Maximian, Maxentius, who had also been ignored in the new official set-up, placed himself at the head of the army in Rome. In the meantime, Maximian relented his earlier resignation and resumed his imperial dignity as an Augustus; while the eastern Augustus, Galerius, and his Cæsar, Maximinus Daias, viewed with disapproval the trend of events. The political stage was well prepared for a bitter civil conflict.

The religious situation was hardly less critical. One who would understand both the popular mind and the psy-chology of the rulers must not forget the important place occupied by religion in Roman thinking among all persons, from the humblest plebeians to the highest officials. Religion and politics were inseparable. The gods sponsored the state and the success of an emperor depended upon the favor of Heaven. The relation was not so much a personal affair as a matter of contract. The persecution of Christianity had been in large measure motivated and justified by this prevailing belief. Christians were "atheists," who refused worship to the ancient deities and thus forfeited the protection of the Empire's divine guardians. Christians, who never questioned the fundamental religious postulate of their persecutors, asserted in defense of their conduct that they were the best friends of the state since they alone worshiped the God who could insure stability and good government to the distressed Roman world. Certainly Constantine, even had he been indoctrinated by no one but Lactantius, must have been familiar with the Christian position on this vital issue of the times.

For a half-dozen years after the death of his father, Constantine remained in undisputed possession of Gaul, taking up his principal place of residence at Arles in the southern part of the Rhône valley. The country was prosperous and peaceful, since neither his father nor he had vigorously pursued the policy of persecution that had been in vogue in Italy and the East since 303 A.D.. In the meantime Constantine married Fausta, daughter of the Augustus Maximian, and gave asylum to the latter when he was forced to flee from enemies in Italy. Shortly afterwards, when Maximian showed a disposition to possess himself of the government in Gaul, Constantine generously permitted the old man to hang himself. At least, so Constantine's Christian admirers later interpreted the son-in-law's disposal of his imperial father-in-law. The outcome of events

in the East had left Galerius and his associate Augustus
Licinius in power, while Maxentius remained safely and
firmly intrenched in Italy with Rome as his capital. In
these territories Christian sentiment was being continuously
alienated by persistent persecution until early in the year
311, when Galerius and Licinius came to terms with Constantine and all three rulers promulgated an edict of toleration for Christians, admonishing them "to pray their God
for our good estate, for that of the commonwealth, and for
their own, that the commonwealth may endure on every
side unharmed and that they may be able to live securely
in their own homes."

How far Constantine had been responsible for initiating
this change of official attitude toward the church, we do not
know. It seems apparent that by this time he had come
to believe that his own previous success might well be
credited to the favor of the Christian God, whose followers
Constantine had refrained from molesting. But the ultimate test of this divinity's power to implement an emperor's ambition was still to be made. When Galerius died
shortly after the edict of toleration had been issued, his
place in the East was taken by Maximinus Daias who continued to persecute the church. At Rome Maxentius was
also loyal to the old gods and trusted in their support to
give him victory over his foes. For political reasons Constantine felt it necessary to eliminate the aggressive Maxentius, and the conflict between these two rivals was to prove
the final demonstration of the efficiency of the Christian's
God in comparison with that of the old Roman deities.

The triumph of Constantine has today become one of
the high lights in Christian history. The emperor had
good reason to feel convinced that his trust in the Divine

Power revered by the Christians had not been misplaced. Within the brief period of two months Italy had been conquered and Maxentius slain. After the victory Constantine and Licinius in a friendly meeting at Milan reaffirmed the policy of religious toleration, making it more explicit and effective. When presently Maximinus Daias was overthrown in the East, the church throughout the whole Empire at last enjoyed full imperial approval. Ten years later its position was made doubly secure, when Constantine removed Licinius and made himself the sole overlord of the entire Mediterranean regions.

Toleration was not the only favor that Constantine bestowed on the church. In his plans for rehabilitating the Empire he gave Christianity a large place and enacted an increasing body of legislation on its behalf. Confiscated ecclesiastical possessions were restored. Christian congregations were recognized as corporations competent to hold property and received funds from the state treasury. The old Roman custom of exempting the priests of religion from distracting public duties was extended to the Christian clergy in order that they might not be drawn away "by any error of sacrilegious negligence from the service due the Deity." This action was justified on the assumption that when the ministers of religion "show greatest reverence to the Deity the greatest benefits accrue to the state." In the year 321 Sunday was made a legal holiday, especially for "all judges and city people and craftsmen." But in the country the kindly disposition of Providence was not to be contravened by idleness on Sunday, for "it frequently happens that no other days are better suited to planting the grain in the furrows or the vines in trenches." Laws against celibacy and childlessness, formerly promulgated to counteract a decline in the population, were suspended in favor of clerical celibates. As a result of enabling legislation and grants from the imperial exchequer, the Christian church under Constantine attained a new dignity in Roman society.

While Christianity was highly honored by Constantine, it was not given exclusive rights in the Empire. All other religions were similarly tolerated in order that every cult might contribute, according to its ability, toward the divine reinforcement of society's well-being. The God of the Christians was now given complete freedom, side by side with all other deities, to demonstrate his effectiveness by functioning without hindrance from persecutors. At Milan in the year 313, Constantine and Licinius had openly declared it to be their purpose "to set in order the conditions of the reverence paid to the Divinity by giving to the Christians and to all others full permission to follow whatever worship any man had chosen, whereby whatever Divinity there is in heaven may be benevolent and propitious to us and to all placed under our authority." The emperors affirmed their reverence for the "Supreme Divinity" as the overruling Providence in all human affairs, however variously or imperfectly this Power might be represented by the different cults in the Empire. In Roman thinking, all gods had their recognized place when they functioned harmoniously for the common good. Neither the exclusiveness of Jewish allegiance to one deity, nor the Greek philosophical dogma of monotheism, fitted easily into the religious psychology of the Romans. All specific divinities were subject to the pragmatic test of efficiency. The God of the Christians had already demonstrated his ability to aid conspicuously the affairs of Constantine, but the emperor had no intention of relinquishing such assistance as other, even lesser, divinities might be able to grant.

While Constantine never abandoned his policy of universal religious freedom, after the year 312 he trusted mainly to Christianity to mediate the help of Divine Providence in preserving the peace and prosperity of his kingdom. This was a serious responsibility for the church. The instrument was far less perfect than the emperor had at first imagined it to be, and he soon felt the necessity of undertaking repairs on the ecclesiastical machinery. Instead of functioning as the agent of peace, the church was itself sometimes rent asunder by dissensions. On more than one occasion this situation irritated and perplexed Constantine. He persisted in his efforts to remedy the defect, although it is doubtful whether he ever fully understood its causes. Yet, as an apostle of unity, he certainly believed himself to be more in accord with the divine will than were the stubborn leaders of conflicting groups who divided Christianity into parties, thus creating "heresies"—in the administrative rather than the theological sense of the word. Refusal to act harmoniously within the institution, not failure to agree in personal beliefs, was the unpardonable sin for the pious Constantine. This being his state of mind, even though he had not been baptized into church membership, he felt no hesitation in chiding schismatics, giving orders to clerics on administrative matters, or addressing even the most august Christian assemblies convened by his authority. As an emperor who without benefit of clergy or sacraments had chosen to serve the Supreme Divinity whom the church professed to worship, Constantine stood as the personification of an imperialized Christianity. And the church, just emerging from the severest of all its persecutions, was too appreciative of its new privileges to question the propriety of the emperor's procedures. He had a genuine zeal for Christianity but not in accordance with full ecclesiastical knowledge. His shortcomings, his heartless murder of relatives including even his capable son Crispus, and the relics of heathenism that adhered to his rule, were readily overlooked in order that his future fame might rest on the glory of his magnificent achievement in placing the church in an impregnable position on the imperial map.

ATHANASIUS

There was one cleric who stoutly refused to bow the knee to Christian emperors. This was Athanasius of Alexandria. The probable date of his birth is the year 293, but nothing is known with certainty about his parentage. Early in his career he became active in the Alexandrian church under its bishop Alexander. He had been ordained a deacon, and apparently stood high in the confidence of his bishop, before Constantine summoned the famous council that met at Nicæa in the year 325. Also, Athanasius was already the author of a remarkable treatise, written in his early twenties, on the *Incarnation of the Word of God*. This shows him to have been of a strongly theological turn of mind, while at the same time he was firmly convinced that the Christian religion was inseparably bound up with the operations of the divinely established sacramental institution. In sentiment and interest he and Constantine were poles apart.

Still other forces had been at work shaping the situation for Athanasius. Ever since the early part of the second century Alexandrian society had been a fertile soil for the growth of divergent opinions and practices among Christians. The bishop of the city, who enjoyed metropolitan prerogatives, found it no easy task to control his neighboring Egyptian bishops and lesser clergy. The recent period of persecution had further upset the orderliness of ecclesiastical procedures. And when Constantine, after the overthrow of Licinius, took up the task of rehabilitating the eastern half of the Empire he found his ideal of Christian peace and unity seriously menaced by strife in Egypt. A dispute that proved particularly acrimonious and far-reaching in its effects had been begun about the year 318, when Arius, an influential presbyter in the Alexandrian church, had openly challenged the logic of his bishop's teaching. In the worship of the Christian congregations, God and Christ were hardly distinguishable in the divine sphere; so far as the rites of the church were concerned, Christ the Son was as truly God as was God the Father whom the Old Testament revealed. As is the custom with bishops, Alexander had the ecclesiastical rather than the logical mind, and went to the extreme of affirming that the Father and the Son were coeternal.

Arius, who had attended a school conducted at Antioch in Syria by a learned Christian, Lucian, was too loyal to Greek philosophical thinking to permit the irrational implications in Alexander's teaching to pass unchallenged. Arius declared that Father and Son could not be coeternal, since a father must be older than a son. Later Arius, in a letter to one of his old schoolmates, gave a picturesque description of the quarrel: "Alexander has driven us out of the city as atheists because we do not concur in what he publicly teaches, namely, 'God is always, the Son is always; as the Father so the Son; the Son coexists unbegotten with God; he is everlastingly begotten; he is the unbegotten begotten; neither by thought nor by any other interval does God precede the Son; always God, always the Son; the Son is of God himself.' . . . To these impieties we cannot listen even though heretics threaten us with a thousand deaths. But we say and believe and have taught and do teach that the Son is not unbegotten, nor in any way part of the unbegotten, nor from any subsistence, but that of his own will and counsel he has subsisted before time and before ages, as perfect God, only-begotten and unchangeable, and that before he was begotten or created or established he was not. For he was not unbegotten. We are persecuted because we say that the Son has a beginning but that God is without beginning."

Thus the battle raged over phrases. Today one may smile at this war of words, but in the ancient world, with its distinctive interests at heart, the issue was one for which representatives of each party were willing to suffer banishment or, if necessary, even death. And it was taken so seriously that in course of time it split Christendom into two rival denominations—one called the Arian and the other the Catholic church—that existed side by side for centuries.

Arius, who was popular, well educated, ascetic in his piety, and persuasive in argument, won a substantial following not only in Egypt but among influential friends in important Christian centers of Asia. The controversy had been gaining strength for six years before Constantine came into possession of the East. From his point of view the eastern churches were virtually in a state of civil war, for which the Christian leaders in Egypt were held chiefly to blame. Already the emperor had learned something about the difficulty of suppressing a schism. In North Africa he had tried to persuade, and then to force, the protesting Donatists to submit to the authority of the bishop Cæcil-

ianus, whom the emperor recognized at Carthage after
episcopal assemblies in the West had decided against the
Donatists. Constantine had even gone to the extreme of
employing soldiers in confiscating the churches of the
schismatics and turning over their property to the imperial
treasury. But he disliked the rôle of persecutor and presently gave it up, leaving the recalcitrants to the judgment
of God—a "most ignominious indulgence," as Augustine a
century later termed the emperor's final action. Undoubtedly this unhappy experience made him more cautious
and temperate when he approached the problem in the East,
but he felt none the less eager to establish harmony.

First, Constantine sent his chief religious adviser, Hosius,
bishop of Cordova in Spain, to negotiate for the peace of
Christianity in Alexandria. When this mission proved un-
successful the emperor decided to call a meeting of bishops
from different churches to obtain an episcopal judgment
that might be enforced by imperial authority. This procedure was a further development of the method that had
previously been used by Constantine in dealing with the
Donatists. But now he determined to make the gathering
representative of all Christendom—an "ecumenical" council, the first of its kind in the history of the church. Passing
over the action of a local synod in Antioch where Arius had
been unequivocally condemned, and anticipating the plans
for another council of eastern clerics at Ancyra where further
condemnation was a foregone conclusion, the emperor
ordered a more comprehensive group to assemble at Nicæa,
near Nicomedia, where the deliberations could be more
easily conducted under imperial supervision.

The council at Nicæa met in the early summer of 325.
A somewhat doubtful tradition states that three hundred

and eighteen bishops attended. At any rate, it was the most pretentious and formidable body of Christian dignitaries that had ever been convened. Although it was "ecumenical," and as such spoke for the whole Christian world, it was predominantly eastern, there being less than a dozen delegates from the West. But Hosius was present, and, as Constantine's spokesman, largely dominated the situation. Athanasius, as a kind of private secretary to his bishop, Alexander, was also there and exerted a far greater influence than the young deacon's ecclesiastical status would have led one to expect. Moreover, he and Hosius entertained very similar sentiments regarding the main theological issue at stake. Neither of them had any sympathy with what might well be called the "modernism" of Arius. Constantine, however, was far more interested in securing general consent to a working agreement than in determining the validity of specific items of dogma. In effect, he demanded of the council that it formulate a statement so phrased and tempered by moderation that all present could append their signatures, even at the cost of suppressing counter personal views and interests. The church, like the state, required the subordination of the individual to the good of the whole.

The assembly caught the spirit of the emperor, and after several weeks of debate in which proposals and counter proposals were presented, agreed to a statement acceptable to the great majority of the extremists of both wings, as well as to the representatives of the center-party. All present, except Arius and one or two of his friends, signed on the dotted line. Christendom now had for the first time in its history a universally authoritative statement of belief—a "Catholic" creed—that might properly be implemented by the power of the state. The formula was not intended, at least by many of those who sponsored it, to be a definitive statement of personal belief clear and logical in every detail, but a general declaration of willingness to refrain from further debate on the main issue raised by Arius. Also, the creed was capable of being interpreted by the individual in a rather free fashion. Thus general assent, which was the end sought by Constantine, had been more fully realized than perhaps he had even dared to hope. The course of action for the emperor was clear; Arius and his obstinate followers were immediately banished. Constantine undoubtedly felt highly gratified over the outcome of the council.

Athanasius, who returned to Alexandria with his bishop, also had reason to feel happy. His cause had triumphed and Arius, the chief agitator, was excluded from the country. At first sight it may have looked like an easy victory for the episcopal authority in Alexandria, but as a matter of fact Athanasius' greatest troubles were still in the future. The agreement reached at Nicæa had not alienated from Arius many of his well-disposed friends in Egypt; they still constituted a powerful minority. Then, too, some twenty-odd bishops were adherents of the so-called Meletian party, a separatist group that had emerged out of the Diocletian persecution. When Alexander died in the year 328, Athanasius was elected to the bishopric, but not without a strong opposition. In the meantime capable supporters of Arius had been active in Asia. Such of them as had signed the Nicene statement, having done so largely to please the emperor, now began the work of undermining his confidence in the validity of the council's action. They were especially skilful in playing politics. Their leader was

Eusebius of Nicomedia, an old school chum of Arius, whose efforts were successful in persuading Constantine to rescind the earlier decree of banishment imposed upon the more persistent Arians. The emperor became persuaded that even Arius was willing to let bygones be bygones, and was ready to return to his religious activities in a spirit of toleration. Athanasius was ordered to receive him back into good standing in the church at Alexandria.

It was now that Athanasius' lifelong struggle against the dominance of emperors over bishops actually began. Arius could not be received on a mere promise of good behavior; he must first whole-heartedly renounce his allegedly erroneous theological opinions and accept the views held by Athanasius, before the latter would receive the heretic into the communion of the church. Thus Athanasius incurred suspicion as the stubborn exponent of factions. At least so it seemed to Constantine, and the Arians were not slow to make capital of the emperor's misgivings. His distrust of Athanasius as an enemy to religious harmony led Constantine in 335 A.D. to summon the Alexandrian bishop to appear before a synod at Tyre to answer the charges of his enemies. He was none too ready to obey but finally came. He did not, however, submit to the decision of the council, but went on to Constantinople where he appealed in person to the emperor whom he seems to have convinced that the proceedings at Tyre were unfair. Yet Athanasius remained a serious obstacle to peace; he was still unwilling to receive Arius even on orders from the emperor. Therefore Athanasius was banished to Trier in Gaul, where he remained until Constantine died in the year 337.

Constantine's three sons inherited his kingdom. Constantius II, who ruled in the East from the start, and over the whole Empire from 350 to 361, was a zealous Arian. Throughout this period Athanasius' difficulties continually multiplied. In 338 he returned to Alexandria, but within two years was forced to leave, making his way to Rome accompanied by two Egyptian monks. Still later he moved to Milan. All the while he was an ardent missionary for Catholicism against Arianism. In the course of the next half-dozen years Constantius II seems to have concluded that the Arian denomination, which he highly favored, would profit more by removing its doughty opponent from the West and allowing him to return to Alexandria. Throughout the next decade Athanasius remained in his old charge unmolested. But the cause he represented was at a low ebb. All around him Arianism was flourishing. Even in the West the Roman bishop, Liberius, under pressure from the emperor, declared himself on the Arian side in 358 A.D., and tradition reports that the venerable Hosius was also forced to commune with the Arians. It was a dark hour for the cause of Athanasius; almost the whole of Christendom seemed enslaved to the imperial will. Conditions became so menacing in Alexandria that Athanasius spent the last five years under Constantius' rule hiding in the Egyptian desert.

Then came the deluge that momentarily threatened to engulf all branches of Christendom. The new emperor, Julian, declared himself opposed to the Christian churches and intent upon restoring the ancient heathen religions. Since universal toleration was, fortunately, made a feature of the new imperial policy, Athanasius was free to return to Alexandria where he spent the remaining twelve years of his career relatively undisturbed. When Julian's rule came to a sudden end in 363, emperors resumed allegiance to the church, favoring Catholicism in the West and Arianism in the East. But the eastern ruler Valens (364-378), although a belligerent Arian, did not seriously interfere with Athanasius. There were other more menacing frontiers than Alexandria that claimed his attention. The aged archbishop expired peacefully in the year 373, the leadership of the Christian cause passing to Basil of Cappadocia in the East and to Ambrose at Milan in the West.

Varying judgments have been passed upon the work of Athanasius. He has most commonly been lauded as the uncompromising champion of orthodox dogma. Such, unquestionably, he was. But his significance for the church of the fourth century was, perhaps, even greater in the sphere of Christianity's relations with the Roman government. He was the one leader of the age who consistently resisted the control of the church by the head of the state. He was not averse to imperializing Christianity, but it was to be an imperialism of creed rather than one of ecclesiastical politics. He has sometimes been accused of entertaining an episcopal obsession motivated by the "will to power." But this judgment does not reveal the inner secret of his life. It remained for a later generation to evolve the idea of an imperial bishop, a development that was the product of the West rather than the East. Athanasius' outstanding contribution to Christianity was his ideal of an infallible ecumenical creed, to which bishops and emperors alike owed unquestioning obedience.

BASIL

Eastern Asia Minor produced several outstanding Christians during the latter part of the fourth century. Three names are especially notable: Gregory of Nazianzus, Basil of Cæsarea (in Cappadocia) and the latter's younger brother, Gregory of Nyssa. They are frequently referred to as the three distinguished "Cappadocians."

The territory of Cappadocia, which had been made a Roman province early in the first century A.D., embraced the upland plain in the eastern section of the peninsula of Asia Minor. Conditions of life in these regions were somewhat distinctive. Commercial enterprise, favored under Roman administration, had resulted in the growth of a few cities, the largest of which was Cæsarea. In the fourth century it was an active business and manufacturing center, the cultural metropolis of the province, with perhaps half a million population. But it hardly rivaled in importance the better known cities of Rome, Carthage, Alexandria, Antioch (in Syria), and Constantinople, which Constantine had made the new capital of the Empire. The country districts in Cappadocia were in possession of large land-owners, who constituted a kind of feudal aristocracy living in prosperity on estates worked by peasants who were virtually bound to the soil. It was from this feudal class, who had leisure and means for acquiring the best education available in the Roman world, that some of Christianity's ablest leaders came. Basil belonged in this category.

The date of Basil's birth is commonly placed about the year 330. He was one of nine surviving children, five sons and four daughters; and his oldest sister, Macrina, of whom a younger brother, Gregory of Nyssa, wrote a charming little biography, was one of the most distinguished women of the ancient church. For three generations the family had been devoted to Christianity. The country had been extensively evangelized by an admiring pupil of Origen, an earlier Gregory surnamed "Thaumaturgus," who in 240

A.D. became bishop at Neocæsarea in the province of Pontus lying north of Cappadocia. For some thirty years he served the church so faithfully that tradition declared he had found only seventeen Christians in the city at the beginning of his ministry, while only seventeen heathen could be found there at the time of the bishop's death.

Basil's father, who bore the same name, was a prosperous lawyer and rhetorician at Cæsarea, and an earnest Christian who owned a large estate in Pontus at Annesi on the river Iris, not far from Neocæsarea. Basil, a frail child, was placed under the care of his paternal grandmother who resided at the family home in Annesi. There he was taught the Christian religion as the grandmother had learned it from Gregory Thaumaturgus. When he reached a suitable age, the youth was brought by his father to Cæsarea for further schooling. He made rapid progress, showing unusual aptitude for both philosophy and rhetoric. Having fully availed himself of such educational facilities as were afforded by Cæsarea, where his studies were carried on under his father's supervision, he was sent to Constantinople. Later, moving on to Athens, he spent five years at the world's most famous university.

Among the students at Athens, Basil found Gregory of Nazianzus, with whom he seems already to have been acquainted, and the two became close friends thoroughly devoted to their studies. At first the sensitive Basil had been unhappy in Athens, where the time-honored custom of hazing freshmen was in vogue, but with Gregory's help he survived the ordeal. Both young men appeared to be destined for a brilliant secular career. But each of them had a Christian background, which even the fascination of their academic pursuits could not entirely obliterate.

Early in the year 356 Basil returned to his native Cæsarea and immediately became a popular teacher of rhetoric. His father had died five years earlier, but his mother Emmelia, and her oldest daughter, Macrina, had successfully managed the extensive family inheritance and still maintained the old home at Annesi. Possessed of an ample patrimony and the finest education the age could offer, Basil's future seemed assured. But this prospect did not furnish his pious mother and sister the complete satisfaction that one might imagine. They had become strongly imbued with ascetic notions. When Macrina's fiancé, to whom her father had betrothed her, suddenly died, she determined to devote herself to a life of perpetual virginity and religious simplicity. Fearing that her talented young brother was in serious danger of succumbing to the blandishments of the world, she rebuked him heartily for his life of vanity. Almost immediately her protest bore fruit and Basil was "converted."

Basil had always been a Christian in the informal sense, although he had not been baptized. But his sympathies had been entirely with the church and apparently his morals were up to standard. His "conversion," therefore, is not to be understood as a turning away from heathenism to the Christian religion. Rather, it meant the abandonment of secular ambition and the adoption of the monastic ideal. A life of simplicity consecrated to meditation, practice in self-discipline, and the service of one's fellows now became Basil's ambition. In one of his *Letters* (No. 223) he depicts the change in his sentiments: "I awoke as from deep sleep, and cast my eyes upon that admirable light of the truth, the Gospel. Then I saw the vanity of the wisdom of the princes of this world, who toil without result. Long I wept over the misery of my life, and prayed that a hand should come and lead me, and teach me the lessons of piety. Then when I had read the Gospel, and learned the best way of arriving at piety was to sell my goods and give them to the poor, and to be no longer anxious about this life, nor allow my soul to be distracted by any sympathy for earthly things, I wanted to find a brother who had chosen that path, that we might pass through the short agitations of life together." Thus began Basil's interest in monastic discipline and charitable activities, the further organization of which constituted one of his chief contributions—probably, indeed, his greatest—to the history of Christianity.

With the scholar's instinct for research, Basil straightway undertook a journey that carried him to parts of Egypt, Syria, Palestine and Mesopotamia in order that he might obtain a first-hand acquaintance with the highly reputed exponents of monasticism in those regions. Filled with admiration for the continent life, he resolved to establish a monastic community for himself and his friends. After some amusing correspondence with his old school friend, Gregory, about the choice of an appropriate location, Basil picked a spot directly across the Iris from Annesi where numerous disciples came to him. He praised the charms of the site but Gregory, who paid him a brief visit, could not endure the place and refused to join the company. With masterly skill Basil organized the life of the community on new lines of practical effectiveness, including both private meditation and active benevolence in contact with the environing society. Within a year's time the foundation was so firmly established that Basil felt at liberty to make a trip to Constantinople to visit a council convened by Constantius to advance the interests of Arianism, with which Basil was not sympathetic.

On returning to Cappadocia, Basil began to take a more active part in ecclesiastical affairs. He broke his friendship with the bishop of Cæsarea, Dianius, by whom Basil had been baptized and ordained a reader in the church, because the bishop was too conciliatory in his attitude to Arian liberalism. When Dianius died some months later, Basil was instrumental in securing the appointment of a certain Eusebius. But the new bishop displayed so much jealousy toward his efficient helper that the latter retired to the seclusion of his monastery on the Iris.

The troubles of the times, and the solicitations of Gregory of Nazianzus, induced Basil to return to the work of the church in Cæsarea, where he was ordained to the priestly office in 364 A.D., and quickly became the most influential person in the diocese. He especially distinguished himself in the great famine of the year 368, of which he gives a vivid account in his homily *On the Famine and Drought*. From his personal resources he purchased provisions for the needy and by his eloquent appeals persuaded the more affluent citizens to follow his example. Two years later, when Eusebius died, Basil secured his own election to the episcopal office which he held until his death on January 1, 379.

Basil's career as bishop was filled with labors and anxieties. Neither the condition of the times nor his own personality was conducive to an easy life. Valens, the eastern ruler and an ardent Arian, did many things to irritate the bishop, whose obedience the emperor was unable to command. Basil's health, never good and now broken by austerities, was wretched. Although still in his forties, he

must have presented the appearance of an octogenarian.
Yet he retained some sense of humor. When a well-mean-
ing friend sent him sweetmeats for Christmas he thanked
him for his folly in making so inappropriate a gift to a
toothless old man who could no longer crunch candy. He
commented on the futility of a month's treatment at the
hot springs by citing the adage: "Warmth does the dead
no good." Fever tortured him sometimes for weeks in
succession, while his unruly liver was a perpetual trouble-
maker. It is not surprising that he occasionally tried the
patience of even his best friends. At one time or another
he incurred the ill-will of some of his most distinguished
episcopal neighbors, and he displayed a rather disdainful
attitude toward Christian leaders in the West. .

In the course of time Basil's weaknesses, that had been
momentarily so irritating, were forgotten, as the full extent
of his enduring work on behalf of Christianity became more
evident. His pronouncements on political and doctrinal
issues were important, and his effectiveness as a preacher
and writer was conspicuous. But his insistence on practical
morality and spiritual sincerity were even more noteworthy.
He vigorously attacked evils within the church, even among
the clergy, where he found simony and laxity in ordinations
all too prevalent. His monastery was not a mere asylum
for the world-weary, but was a training camp to prepare
good soldiers for service on the battlefield of life. He
made monasticism a working ally of the ecclesiastical organization, and particularly responsible for ministering to the
poverty and suffering of needy humanity at large. Basil's
monastic establishment near Cæsarea, probably modeled
after a similar but less pretentious undertaking carried on
by his friend Eustathius at Sebaste, was called the "New

City," and was so elaborate that it was said to have threatened the prestige of the capital, Cæsarea. The buildings included a fine church, with a residence for the clergy, apartments for needy travelers, hospitals for the care of the sick, a workhouse for the unemployed, and other provisions for hospitality and charity. In modern phraseology, it might be termed a great charitable and social settlement. Some of the monks were trained to be village bishops who, under Basil's guidance, set up like centers in their own territories.

It may almost be said that Basil had launched a new Christian movement by the side of the official church, yet without injecting the spirit of rivalry into the situation. His conception of Christianity's task as an organized endeavor was more all-embracing than anyone before his day had realized. He was as resolute as Athanasius in resisting political domination over the church, and in the main he stood firmly by the principle of ecumenical orthodoxy in dogma. But none of his predecessors or contemporaries perceived so clearly as did he that if true Christianity was to be saved for the world by which it had been formally adopted it must be more thoroughly organized as a way of religious living. Instead of individuals withdrawing from a contaminating environment to cultivate in solitude a worthy piety, the church must fortify itself against defeat by systematically and diligently socializing the monastic ideal. If Basil had been asked to define his notion of an imperial Christianity he might fittingly have phrased it in terms of a holy way of daily living in service to God and needy humanity to be made universally regnant throughout the Roman Empire.

Ambrose

The outstanding leader of western Christendom during the last quarter of the fourth century was Ambrose of Milan. As a young man he had not planned to enter the ecclesiastical profession, although he had been reared in a Christian atmosphere and was genuinely interested in the church, especially its Catholic branch. His father, a Roman of high station, was Pretorian Prefect of Gaul, where Ambrose had been born about the year 340, probably at Trier. After the early death of his father the widow with her three children moved to Rome where the family lived amid associations befitting its rank. Ambrose received an excellent education in both Latin and Greek literature. Following in the footsteps of his father, he studied law by way of preparing himself for an administrative career. Evidently Christian influence dominated the family circle, for his sister Marcellina dedicated herself to a life of virginity while Ambrose was still a young man and when he became a bishop she proved to be one of his most efficient helpers in the work of the church at Milan.

While still in his twenties, Ambrose was appointed to an important position as assistant to the Pretorian Prefect of Italy. Shortly afterwards he was made Consul, and placed in charge of the government of the northern section of Italy—the provinces of Liguria and Æmilia—with his official residence at Milan. He early won distinction as a just and capable governor whom the people trusted and admired. When Auxentius, the bishop at Milan, died, orderly procedure in the election of his successor required diligent attention from the officials of the state. In those days the choice of a new bishop was the business of the

Christian populace, and the excitement incident to the occasion was likely to develop riotous proportions as rival parties sought to secure the position for their favored candidates. As governor, Ambrose went to the church to address the assembly in the interests of concord and suddenly found himself the popularly acclaimed candidate for the episcopal office. With becoming modesty he demurred; he had not yet been baptized, much less had he been trained theologically and ecclesiastically for the discharge of clerical duties. But the people were insistent and Ambrose yielded. The neighboring Italian bishops and the emperor having indicated their approval, Ambrose was baptized and eight days later was consecrated bishop. The generally accepted date for his appointment is December 7, 374, although there are some reasons for believing that the year may have been 373.

Ambrose found himself almost immediately launched upon a sea of troubles. Milan was now the political capital of Italy and its ruling bishop had to discharge responsibilities that were even more serious than those devolving upon Ambrose's illustrious contemporary, Damasus of Rome, whose problems were by no means insignificant. It was fortunate indeed for the history of the western church that it could avail itself of a man with Ambrose's moral earnestness and administrative skill to guide its destinies during this crucial period.

Certainly Ambrose was not utterly unaware of the difficulties that lay in his path. His sympathies were emphatically with the Catholic section of Christianity, as opposed to the Arian branch, whose power under imperial favor had rapidly grown even in the West. Ambrose's predecessor in the episcopal see at Milan had been an Arian, a fact that probably had not a little to do with determining Ambrose to accept the office. Although the western emperor, Valentinian, gave his preference to Catholicism, his wife, Justina, and his eastern colleague, Valens, were zealous for Arianism. Also the Goths, who had already filtered into the western Roman world through enlistment in the army and peaceful migrations, were disposed to think with some racial pride of Arianism as their type of Christianity. They cherished the memory of Ulfilas, a missionary who, under Arian auspices at Constantinople, had been consecrated bishop of the Goths in the year 348. For upwards of thirty years he carried on his work of converting the Goths, for whom he made a translation of the Scriptures in their tongue and thus laid the foundation for a future German literature. There were several Arian bishops even in Roman territory when Ambrose entered office. He was fully aware of the menace to Christianity's unity, a situation that would naturally be repulsive to his administrative type of mind.

There were still other serious obstacles to be overcome. Christian leaders were always liable to dictation from the emperor and his court. It needed a man of Ambrose's political experience to handle with delicacy and firmness problems that were becoming ever more critical in the relations between state and church. Then, too, especially in the West, the pagan cults were far from quiescent, and a slowly decaying political authority was unable to hold them in check without the help of a new Christian statesmanship such as Ambrose represented to a marked degree. The bishop's abilities were put to a severe test on all three of these battle fronts—Arianism, imperial aggressiveness and pagan revivalism. Numerous incidents in the life of Ambrose illustrate various phases in his leadership of the Catholic church in conflict with these triple enemies.

The suppression of the Arian church was one of Ambrose's greatest concerns. Although he preached and wrote against its distinctive doctrines, he trusted less to the efficacy of his theological arguments than to his success in procuring condemnatory legislative action. This procedure was more in line with his training as a lawyer and an administrator. Shortly after establishing himself in his episcopal office he took an active part in a synod at Sirmium, where he effected the overthrow of some of his Arian opponents. But the events of the next few years retarded somewhat his progress. The western emperor, who heartily supported Ambrose, died in the autumn of 375, and the bishop had now to make his position secure with the new emperor, Gratian. This effort finally proved successful. In the summer of 379 Ambrose had the satisfaction of witnessing the issuance of an imperial decree at Milan condemning all heretics. The next year the edict was made more explicit and urgent. The government would no longer tolerate a divided church: "According to the apostolic discipline and evangelical doctrine we believe in the deity of the Father and the Son and the Holy Spirit of equal majesty. Those who follow this law we command shall be comprised under the name of Catholic Christians; but others indeed we require, as insane and raving, to bear the infamy of heretical teaching. Their gatherings shall not receive the name of churches. They are to be smitten first by the divine punishment and after that by the vengeance of our indignation, which has the divine approval."

The promulgation of an imperial decree did not necessarily mean its enforcement, especially amid the unsettled political conditions of that age. The temporary victory for Ambrose was, however, very gratifying, and he urged Gratian, who now seemed thoroughly subservient to the bishop's will, to attack the stronghold of paganism at Rome. Gratian, accordingly, canceled the revenues that had customarily been permitted to the priestly colleges and vestal virgins at Rome, and he further ordered the removal of the statue to Victory which stood on an altar in the senate chamber to symbolize Rome's divine glory. But the following year Gratian, while attempting to suppress a revolt in Gaul, was killed at Lyons. He was succeeded by his half-brother Valentinian II, a mere boy, whose mother, Justina, acted as regent. Residing at Milan, they were in close contact with Ambrose who in the year 383 undertook for them a diplomatic mission to the court of the usurper, Maximus of Gaul.

The affairs of Ambrose prospered for a year. A request of the Roman senate for the restoration of the altar of Victory was denied, notwithstanding the eloquence of the distinguished Symmachus; and Ambrose made a second visit on business of state to the court of Maximus. But the next three years constituted, perhaps, the most trying period in Ambrose's entire career. Justina was at heart an Arian, as were many members of her court and the Goths in the imperial army. The legislation of Gratian had denied them the right to assembly, but Justina ordered that a certain church, the Portian Basilica, should be given them for use. When Ambrose protestingly withheld his consent, the empress proposed to take the building by force. Since the bishop had no police to protect the ecclesiastical property, he camped for several days with his faithful followers at the church and successfully resisted dislodgment. It was at this time, it is said, that he composed three of his greatest hymns and taught the congregation to sing antiphonally to inspire them to endurance.

Bickerings between the representatives of Justina and the bishop continued until the usurper Maximus, and Eugenius, the leader of the revolting pagan party, threatened to invade Milan and stable their horses in its great cathedral. Then timely help arrived. Theodosius, the eastern emperor, appeared upon the scene, conquered and slew Maximus, and supplanted the troublesome Justina. Since the new ruler proved as amenable to the wishes of the bishop as Gratian had been, the supremacy of Ambrose was once more established. His anxieties did not immediately evaporate, but under imperial protection he was able to enforce with increasing effectiveness his policy of subjugating both pagans and Arians.

In Milan, Ambrose and Theodosius now stood unchallenged, and were practically autonomous in their respective spheres of church and state. Between them the relationship was one of mutual admiration and devotion. As friends they were peers, but in the event of a conflict of wills, would it be the bishop or the emperor who would give way? Heretofore emperors had always dominated bishops. When one considers the vast debt of gratitude due Theodosius for the help he had rendered Ambrose, one might readily predict that Theodosius would play the victorious rôle of a second Constantine. But times had changed. Barely had Theodosius established his supremacy over the entire Empire by defeating Maximus, when he learned that he was face to face with another potentate, not so easily to be overthrown, in the person of Ambrose.

News reached the emperor that some overzealous Christians, urged on by their bishop in one of the towns of Mesopotamia under Theodosius' jurisdiction, had burned a Jewish synagogue. Angered by this vandalism, Theodosius ordered the rebuilding of the structure with money to be provided from the funds of the offending bishop. Ambrose immediately objected. The emperor refused to grant him a personal interview, but the bishop wrote a letter demanding that an expenditure of Christian money should not be ordered without the consent of its proper guardians, a council of bishops. In all matters of religion the "ministers of the Lord" should be consulted, just as in affairs of state the emperor consulted his ministers. When this appeal failed the bishop played a higher card. Ambrose, it must be remembered, was priest and preacher for the worshiping congregation where the emperor received his spiritual guidance and training for the salvation of his immortal soul. From his pulpit in the church, with Theodosius before him, Ambrose preached one of his powerful sermons on the duty of rulers to protect the body of Christ—the Catholic church—if the Empire was to enjoy the protection of Christ. Then Ambrose dramatically refused to approach the altar to offer the holy sacrifice until Theodosius gave a positive promise to withdraw his demand upon the Mesopotamian bishop. Under this pressure from Heaven the emperor yielded.

Still later, in a burst of anger over a local uprising at Thessalonica, Theodosius ordered a wholesale slaughter of the citizens, among whom many Christians perished. Again Ambrose rose up in righteous indignation, declaring that he could not offer the holy sacrifice in the presence of the unrepentant imperial sinner. Until Theodosius had performed the necessary penance he must remain away from the church where the holy sacrifice was celebrated for the benefit of the faithful. Again Theodosius yielded. He made the humiliating display of public repentance demanded by the bishop before restoring the emperor to communion. What Constantine would have done under similar circumstances one can only imagine. Certainly he was not as good a Christian as Theodosius—if fear of Heaven's vengeance enacted by God through the mediation of a bishop is taken to be a test of genuine Christianity. At last an emperor had bowed the knee to the church; imperial authority had passed to Christianity.

CHAPTER VI

CHRISTIAN LUMINARIES IN A DARK- ENING AGE

By the year 400 Roman imperialism had come to a part- ing of the ways. The forces of disintegration had been gaining momentum for over two centuries, notwithstanding the heroic efforts of capable administrators like Diocletian and Constantine to prevent dissolution. After the death of Theodosius in 395 A.D., there was never again to be a po- litically unified Mediterranean world. Justinian, who ruled from Constantinople in the sixth century (527-565 A.D.), recaptured North Africa, Italy and a part of Spain, in an attempt to restore the ancient Empire, but the struggle was in vain. Destiny had decreed that the domains once ruled by Augustus should no longer be embraced under one sover- eign. The eastern Empire was to endure for another thou- sand years, but a very different political future was in store for the West.

Christianity remained the most stable unifying force throughout the Mediterranean lands. But the church, al- though claiming solidarity in the name of an overruling Providence, could not wholly resist the processes of social degeneration. Even in the East, Christendom was unable to maintain organic unity. The rivalry of great patri- archates, such as those of Alexandria, Antioch and Con- stantinople, was a constant source of friction; while bitter theological disputes resulted in the formation of incompatible groups who constituted themselves into separate communions not unlike the competing denominations that have been so conspicuous a feature in American Christianity.

The western churches suffered less from internal dissensions, but were very seriously affected by the general dissolution of the contemporary social order under the impact of the barbarian invaders who swarmed into Italy, Gaul, Spain and North Africa from beyond the Danube and the Rhine. The once luminous star of Roman imperialism was rapidly sinking in the West. Ancient civilization, the best elements of which had been extensively incorporated into Christianity, was entering upon a kind of arctic night that later historians were to call the "Dark Ages."

In the initial years of this declining period of cultural history Christianity produced three men of outstanding fame, who had no peers in their own day and who were not to be excelled throughout many succeeding centuries. These notable persons were John Chrysostom, the brilliant pulpiteer; Jerome, the distinguished scholar; and Augustine, the eminent theologian.

JOHN CHRYSOSTOM

John is better known as Chrysostom, meaning "goldenmouthed," a name given to him by admirers of his eloquence years after his death. At the time of his birth, about 347 A.D., his father was a military man of high rank and head of the army quartered at Antioch. While John was yet an infant his father died, leaving an estate ample for the support of the family and the education of the children. There seems to have been an older sister, who probably died in childhood. The mother continued to reside in Antioch where John received both secular and religious training.

The young widow, a pious and intelligent woman, gave her undivided attention to the education of her son and the conservation of his father's estate, while she possessed in her own right a dowry from her parents sufficient for the needs of the bereaved family.

John's mother had many cares. She managed indolent and perverse servants, she thwarted the designs of scheming relatives, she maintained her Christian equanimity in spite of provocations from rude and greedy tax-gatherers, she resisted the appeals of eager suitors, and she refused to alleviate the hard lot of the widow by contracting a second marriage, all for the sake of her son's welfare. She drew her comfort from two sources of help. One was the assistance she received "from above" and the other was the memory of her deceased husband whose exact image she saw afresh in the features of her child. On him she lavished the wealth of her affections, she provided money for his schooling, she nourished his religious life under the warm sunshine of her rich spiritual personality, and when the son chafed somewhat under the restraint of her appeals she could heartily assure him that there was no person in all the world to whom his reputation was more dear than to her. As John grew to manhood he combined in his character the dauntless temper that may have been an inheritance from his soldier-father, Secundus, and the moral strength of his mother, Anthusa.

Antioch already was widely celebrated as a center of both heathen and Christian learning. But the best schools in the Roman Empire were still in heathen hands, and at Antioch the most famous teacher of Greek rhetoric was Libanius. John, who became his exceptionally capable pupil, bore throughout life the stamp that had been placed upon him by this illustrious pagan orator. Another of his teachers was Andragathius, a philosopher. But his impression upon the boy was far less abiding, for John, like Basil of Cappadocia, inclined to the conviction that "philosophy" in its highest form was to be attained through the contemplative life of the monk rather than in the classroom of a university. John had a school friend, another Basil, who was like-minded. These two serious youths were much together, and frequently talked of their plans for the future. In both of them zeal for the monastic ideal had early been kindled.

After completing their formal education John had been more tardy than his friend in embracing ascetic discipline. John's sensible mother seems to have been a deterrent influence. In his treatise *On the Priesthood* he tells the pathetic story of how she once pled with him to remain by her side instead of wandering off into remote places to live the life of a hermit. Reminding him of the sacrifices she had made on his behalf, she begged that he would not inflict upon her a second bereavement such as she had suffered in the death of her husband. She besought him not "to rouse afresh that grief which has now sunk to rest. Only wait for my death; perhaps I shall depart ere long. They who are young look forward to a distant old age, but we who are grown old have nothing to wait for but death. When you have consigned me to the ground and mingled my remains with your father's bones, then set out on long travels and sail whatever sea you desire." It seemed to the son that his mother was distracting him with worldly cares by insisting that he remain at home to manage the business affairs of the family estate. But, temporarily, he complied with his mother's wishes. He was now slightly past thirty years of age, and his mother seems to have been about twenty years older.

Antioch was not the most propitious spot for a prosperous and well-educated young man to lead a sedat_y religious life. Although half the population may h_ r_ been at least nominally Christian, the atmosphere of u_e civic life was heavily loaded with the seductive aromas of heathen customs and pleasures. John's education had especially fitted him for the legal profession. We do not know that he ever took up seriously this calling, but he says explicitly that it once had been his custom to frequent regularly the law courts and that he took pleasure in attending the theater. These activities had interrupted somewhat association with his old companion, Basil, who remained closeted with his books and never visited the market-place. But the abiding friendship finally matured in a plan by which the two were to go into monastic retirement. This was the moment when John, divulging his purpose to his mother, drew forth her solicitous protest.

Still other influences had been effective in shaping John's career. Life in the home had made him familiar with the Bible, and Christian teachers of Antioch were his friends. In the city at this time there were three rival Christian movements—the radical Arians, the extreme Catholics, and the central party—each with its own bishop and independent ecclesiastical organization. The last of these groups was presided over by Bishop Meletius. Probably Anthusa belonged to the Meletian community. At any rate, John attracted the attention of Meletius, who tutored the young man in Christianity, baptized him about the year 368, and ordained him a reader in the church. Piety now became a serious business for John, who in the year 374 withdrew to the mountains in the neighborhood of Antioch. For six years he remained in monastic seclusion, rejoicing in his self-inflicted privations, for which he paid the penalty of broken health and a permanently deranged digestion.

In 381 A.D., to save his life, John returned to Antioch. Meletius was delighted to have him back as a helper in the church and, before setting out to attend a council at Constantinople, ordained John a deacon. The bishop died while at Constantinople and his successor, Flavian, elevated John to the priesthood. This was in the year 386.

Almost immediately John became famous. As a priest he was privileged to preach, and his sermons were the marvel of the age. He had lost none of his zeal for pious living, but he transferred it from the cloister into the daily activities of his congregation. With apostolic fervor, but in the language of the finished orator, he thundered against the sins of the people, and exalted the pure moral and spiritual ideals required by a genuine Christianity. People packed the church and hung so intently on the preacher's golden words that pickpockets easily plied their trade during his sermon, while sometimes the audience broke out in tumultuous applause at his magnificent periods. But his head was not in the least turned by this triumph. He did not cease to upbraid his hearers for their unwillingness to practice the precepts he inculcated, and he lamented their praise of his rhetoric when they failed to perceive the spiritual truth he sought to impart.

As John's fame spread, Constantinople coveted his services. Quite against his will he was made patriarch at the capital in the year 397. This was in reality a calamity for John. Apart from his eloquence, he was utterly without qualifications for the position. His uncompromising ethical sincerity made no distinction between the frailties of a street-sweeper and those of an empress. His sharp shafts of rebuke were hurled with unerring aim alike at both. This the populace enjoyed, but the imperial court and the easy-going rich, whom he mercilessly flayed, could not endure his fiery oratory. Socially also, he was quite out of place. His personal attachment to the ascetic life, and his severity with the subordinate clergy, did not suit well the gay life of the fashionable eastern metropolis; while his dyspepsia made him both a poor entertainer and an impossible guest at a stylish banquet. As an ecclesiastical administrator he was sadly lacking in experience. The manner in which he interfered with neighboring episcopal sees under his patriarchal jurisdiction and beyond, to denounce and correct glaring evils, only augmented the fires of hate. A multitude of enemies awaited an opportune moment to take their revenge. Not least among them was the shifty eastern emperor, Anastasius, with his wilful Frankish wife Eudoxia.

Theophilus, the jealous patriarch of Alexandria, provided the first occasion for John's enemies to attempt his downfall. Theophilus was a powerful ecclesiastic, whose influence extended widely in the East. One of his distinctions lies in the fact that he had secured from the civil authorities an order to destroy the famous temple of Serapis, with its great library, in Alexandria. Another of his great enterprises was the overthrow of the noted Origen's reputation as a theologian. At the time, Egypt was full of monks, many of them being students and admirers of Origen's writings. Monks were often a thorn in the side of an archbishop, and Theophilus decided on drastic action against a group that had given him greatest offense. Following a synod in Alexandria that had declared against the teachings of Origen, Theophilus appealed to the prefect for soldiers to make an attack by night upon the monks in the district of Nitria. Four of the leaders of the monks, known as the "Tall Brothers," fled to Constantinople to seek the protection of the patriarch John.

In the meantime an estrangement had arisen between John and the empress, a royal lady with violent likes and dislikes and an inordinate ambition for apparent piety. While John had been absent for three months working on ecclesiastical reforms in Asia, where he had discharged numerous members of the clergy and suppressed much corruption, he had left a certain Severianus in charge at Constantinople. But the man had fallen out with John's trusted archdeacon. On his return John reviewed the difficulty and gave judgment against Severianus, whose sermons had proved especially satisfactory to the empress. She was, naturally, much displeased with the patriarch's action. The arrival of the Tall Brothers gave her an opportunity to rebuff John. He had received them with courtesy, but refused them communion while the shadow of heresy still hung over their heads. When they appealed to the empress as she was riding along the street one day in her chariot, she straightway took the initiative in having Theophilus called to Constantinople for trial on a charge of calumny and persecution.

This action compromised John's position and went quite beyond any intention on his part to become involved in a quarrel with the patriarch of Alexandria. Nor was he any match for Theophilus when it came to a game of ecclesiastical politics. The first move of Theophilus was to secure the aid of his friend Epiphanius of Cyprus who enjoyed a great reputation for piety and orthodoxy. With a large following of bishops and clergy Epiphanius went to Constantinople where he set at defiance John's authority by ordaining a deacon, and then by conferences and addresses tried to persuade the populace and the clergy to make a pronouncement against Origen's views, an action that John had refused to take in the case of the Tall Brothers. But Epiphanius, having failed to accomplish his purpose, retired from the scene before Theophilus arrived. The long-dead Origen had no real enemies in Constantinople, a city founded almost a century after the great scholar had passed away.

Theophilus, awake to the situation, dropped the theological issue and ignored the Tall Brothers. Instead, he preferred trumped-up charges against John, whom he desired above everything else to discredit. Theophilus was quite without rights in John's jurisdiction, but neither propriety nor justice was allowed to interfere with the schemes of the Alexandrian patriarch so long as the imperial authorities did not intervene. Theophilus had gathered thirty-six bishops among his followers and still others from Asia had been summoned hither by command of the emperor. It seemed a grand opportunity for all persons who disliked John to vent their spleen. Yet he had his friends, among whom were forty bishops as well as large numbers of the populace in Constantinople. Consequently Theophilus thought it wise to assemble his followers outside the city, beyond the Bosphorus, at a place called "The Oak," in the neighborhood of Chalcedon. Although this synod four times ordered John to appear before it, he persistently refused to obey the summons. Then he was formally condemned, but the attempt to supplant him in Constantinople resulted in violent rioting and bloodshed. In order to calm the tumult, John temporarily withdrew from the city. While the conflict still raged a severe earthquake that shook even the walls of the imperial palace so alarmed the superstitious empress that the court yielded to the clamors of the people and John was reinstated in triumph.

John's good fortune was short-lived. His indomitable spirit had not been broken, nor was his loyalty to righteousness impaired. He was still the deadly enemy of all those frivolities and vices that characterized the life of the pleasure-loving capital. Scarcely two months passed before John was again in trouble. The effect of the earthquake on the temper of the empress had worn off. She had a silver statue of herself mounted on a porphyry column set up opposite the church of St. Sophia and the hubbub raised by the pagan populace around the memorial from time to time disturbed the services in the church. John complained to the prefect, who reported the matter to the empress in a way that was none too favorable to the patriarch. John may not have used the exact language attributed to him, but the tenor of his criticism can hardly be doubted. For a long time he had heartily disapproved of the conduct of the empress and her servile court clergy. They reminded him of the priests of Baal who "ate at Jezebel's table," and she seemed all too like a second Herodias seeking the head of another John.

With the hostility of the imperial court now restored, John's enemies succeeded in convening another synod. This time no attempt was made to assail his unimpeachable character. Safer ground was chosen for his enemies' attack; he was accused of ecclesiastical irregularity. According to a canon enacted by a council at Antioch in 341 A.D., it was illegal for a bishop who had fled to return to office without the approval of a synod. This legislation, so it was alleged, had been violated by John when he came back to Constantinople after the earthquake. The fact that the council in question had been an Arian assembly, and that John in resuming his see had simply obeyed an imperial order, did not prevent his enemies from pressing their charge. They had their way. The emperor gave his consent to hostile action against John. Soldiers invaded the church and treated with brutal violence the faithful worshipers. Twice an attempt was made upon the life of John, whose removal was finally decreed. Not desiring further bloodshed, he quietly submitted. Terrible riots in Constantinople followed, resulting in the burning of the magnificent cathedral itself, but John was not personally to blame for the disasters. Bound as a convict in chains, he was transported to Cucusus in Armenia in 404 A.D., and three years later died while being removed to a more secluded and inhospitable place northeast of the Black Sea. His dying words were: "Thanks be to God for all things."

John, driven from the most coveted episcopate in the East and dying an exile, lived on illustriously in Christian memory. He wielded a skilful pen as well as an eloquent tongue. Even from his remote place of banishment he carried on an extensive correspondence and exerted a wide influence. Like the Apostle Paul, John's strength of character shining through his words and deeds, rather than his bodily presence, made him significant. Yet he must have been a picturesque figure in the pulpit. Piercing, deep-set eyes gleamed beneath a high and wrinkled brow crowned by a bald head. His pale and shrunken face ended in a pointed short-bearded chin. He was small of stature with the emaciated frame of an ascetic and long arms that gave him, as he says, the appearance of a spider. But his soul was that of a giant.

John Chrysostom is the brightest luminary of the eastern church, and his light shines all the more glowingly because of the gloom of mediocrity already gathering about the heads of its political and episcopal potentates. He was its most illustrious preacher, not simply because he was a master of words or a vigorous debater of theological issues, but, above all, because his sermons were aflame with moral sincerity and spiritual power. On the written page they survived to inspire future generations of preachers. John may have been tactless at times, oversevere in his judgments of others, and sadly lacking in worldly wisdom. But no one can justly accuse him of disloyalty to his moral ideals. He was too ingenuous to practice the chicanery of the ecclesiastical politician; he insisted on making religion a way of noble living to be pursued by all, rich and poor, plebeian and prince; and under no circumstance would he abandon duty to God for the service of emperors. His memory remained a great beacon light on the eastern horizon of Christendom.

JEROME

Jerome was a westerner, born of Catholic parents at Stridon in Dalmatia, around the year 347. Our information about the family is meager. There are occasional references to a maternal aunt, a grandmother, a sister and a brother. The family estates must have been extensive, for their sale furnished Jerome with a substantial sum to defray the expenses of his monastery at Bethlehem, in spite of the fact that the ancestral property had suffered from the incursion of the Goths who destroyed Stridon in the year 377. Probably his parents had been killed at that time.

Like John Chrysostom, Jerome formed a close friendship with a boyhood companion, Bonosus, of the same age and social status. After finishing their elementary studies in Stridon they went to Rome to complete their education in grammar and rhetoric. Jerome must have proved himself an apt pupil, for he acquired a remarkable mastery of the Latin language and a keen taste for its finest literature, acquisitions that equipped him for the distinctive service he was later to render to Christianity. On leaving Rome, Bonosus and Jerome paid a visit to Gaul, residing for some-time at Trier. Whether it was a desire to atone for youthful dissipations or only an excess of early piety that prompted their action, both decided on a life of asceticism. Jerome felt that in a world filled with temptations complete renunciation offered him the only sure way of escape.

The Christian scenes and associations in Rome had vividly impressed the sensitive young Jerome, who presented himself for baptism before his student days had ended. Later he describes the effect of visits often made to the catacombs: "At Rome in my youth when I was devoting myself to liberal studies I was accustomed to visit on Sunday, along with comrades of the same age and occupation, the tombs of the apostles and martyrs. Frequently we entered the crypts excavated deep under ground and presenting to visitors on both sides long walls with entombed bodies. Everything there is so gloomy that one sees almost fulfilled the prophetic saying, 'Let them descend alive into the lower regions.' A light coming from above tempered a little the horror of the darkness. It was not so much a window as an opening allowing the descent of daylight. By walking with short steps one then returned immersed in a blackness of night which recalled to us the line of Virgil, 'Everywhere horror and silence itself terrified our souls.' "

After returning from Gaul, Jerome resided for a time at Aquileia at the head of the Adriatic Sea and attached himself to a group of persons who practiced a rigid self-discipline under the leadership of Chromatius who was later to become bishop of Aquileia. When, for some unknown reason, the company was suddenly dissolved, Jerome decided to journey to the East where monks were more numerous and popular. A few companions joined him, but two of them died on the way and one returned home before they reached Antioch. This was in the year 374.

At Antioch, Jerome fell ill with a severe attack of fever. His friends thought him dead and were making ready for his burial when suddenly he revived and narrated a marvelous vision experienced in his delirium. He had seen himself dragged before the judgment seat in the world beyond the grave. When interrogated by the judge he declared himself a Christian, to which he heard the terrifying reply: "Thou liest, thou art a Ciceronian, not a Christian, 'for where thy treasure is there is thy heart also.' " Then he was led away and severely scourged. Begging for mercy, he promised never again to own or read worldly books. He pledged himself henceforth to study the books of God with even greater zeal than he had formerly shown for the books of men. He had carried his classical library to Antioch, and evidently he did not immediately dispose of the precious possession. Much less could he eliminate from the texture of his mind the classical heritage which his education had planted therein, although he now devoted himself with tireless energy to Scriptural studies. Thanks to his determination, he won enduring fame as a Christian scholar.

On recovering his health Jerome, pursuant to his new resolution, seems to have composed a commentary on the prophet Obadiah, a premature effort which he later excused by quoting Scripture: "When I was a child, I spoke and I thought as a child." He was mentally so constituted that he could never become a dilettante; sound scholarship was the only foundation on which he was content to build. He applied to himself the rule he later imposed on others: "Spend much time in learning what you are to teach." Therefore he plunged into fresh studies, first in Greek, then in Hebrew, and ultimately in Aramaic. At the same time the desire for a life of rigid self-discipline grew upon him. Leaving his friends and his cultural opportunities in Antioch, he attached himself to a monastic community in the desert of Chalcis fifty miles distant. There he remained three years, enduring excruciating physical discomfort relieved only by his joy in intellectual pursuits. But even this pleasure was tempered by the agonies of learning a new and unattractive language. He received regular instruction in Hebrew from a learned Jewish Christian who taught him "harsh and guttural words" that contrasted sharply with the fluent eloquence of Cicero or the charming gentility of Pliny.

Although still in his early thirties, Jerome's monastic life had proved so menacing to his health that he was forced to return to Antioch where the bishop ordained him to the priesthood, an honor that Jerome did not covet. In fact it was virtually imposed upon him; he never undertook the discharge of either pastoral or liturgical functions. A year later, in 380, he went to Constantinople to hear the brilliant

Gregory of Nazianzus, then the patriarch, from whom Jerome learned further skill in biblical exegesis. He busied himself also with literary labors, composing his famous *Chronicle* modeled after the similar book of the first church historian, Eusebius of Cæsarea, whose work Jerome revised and brought down to the year 378. He also displayed a growing enthusiasm for the scholarly writings of Origen, especially his homilies on Scripture. As Cicero had been the great mediator of Greek philosophy to the Romans in the first century B.C., Jerome now undertook the task of rendering Christianity's most distinguished Greek philosopher, Origen, into the Latin tongue. In rapid succession thirty-seven of his homilies on certain of the prophets were translated before the close of the year 381.

The next year Jerome was back in Rome. His fame had preceded him. Damasus, the pope, welcomed him heartily as a helper and literary adviser. The friendship between the two men was so close, and Jerome's services to the church were so remarkable, that his elevation to the papacy when the aged Damasus should die seemed a foregone conclusion. But the Roman community was not yet ready to enthrone a monk in the papal chair. Although Jerome had left the desert, he had not in the least relaxed his admiration for the monastic ideal, and even in Rome he carried on a vigorous propaganda for the ascetic life. In the cours. of time this ardor proved his undoing.

There were several devout and high-born matrons in Rome who were strongly inclined toward ascetic discipline and charitable activity before Jerome returned to the city. Almost immediately he became their mentor. Under influences derived from Athanasius, a certain Marcella, reputed to have been one of the most beautiful ladies of the day, had already converted her home on the Aventine into a place of assembly where pious women now gathered regularly, with Jerome as their guide, to study Scripture, meditate on holy things, and discipline themselves in the rigors of the consecrated life. These ladies, well-to-do and highly educated, delighted to read the prophets and sing the Psalms in the original Hebrew, the sacred language in which Jerome had become an expert. Their intelligent questions tested, and sometimes baffled, his skill in interpretation. But intellectual pursuits were not their only interest. They, too, welcomed lessons in self-discipline, and were ready to spend themselves and their means in humble service for the sick and the poor. Celibacy, prayer, fasting and other austerities were highly exalted as ideals and diligently pursued.

Praise of celibacy and its vigorous advocacy by the group of women who associated themselves with Marcella, seem to have contributed most immediately to Jerome's unpopularity. The attractions of the convent threatened with extinction some of Rome's most notable families, a prospect that even many Christians deplored. About this time a Christian named Helvidius came to the defense of matrimony as an ideal higher than perpetual virginity. He built his argument on gospel passages referring to Mary's life in wedlock, when other children had been borne by her after the birth of Jesus. Apparently Helvidius held the motherhood of Mary in a continuing family life to be especially worthy of emulation. But not so Jerome, who revolted at the notion of Mary's bearing children to Joseph—the "brothers" of Jesus must have been cousins, or close relatives. In righteous indignation Jerome poured out the vials of his wrath on Helvidius, who had "soiled with

slime" the holy name of the Blessed Virgin and "fouled the
sanctuary of the Holy Spirit by presumptuously making a
whole cartload of brothers and sisters issue therefrom."
This crude language was not likely to improve Jerome's
standing with many Christian families at Rome.

When it came to a matter of vilifying the fashionable
married ladies at Rome, Jerome exercised no restraint over
his vocabulary of vituperation. He ridiculed them for daub-
ing their cheeks with rouge, charcoaling their eyebrows and
using belladonna to make their eyes sparkle. With their
faces plastered to an excessive whiteness they looked like
pagan idols, while a careless tear running down the cheek
left in its trail a hideous furrow. They tried to conceal
their years by piling up false hair on their heads, they
sought to disguise the wrinkles of age by polishing up their
faces with cosmetics and then acting like a bunch of school-
girls before their grandsons. Such care of the flesh definitely set aside the apostolic warning that "those who are in
the flesh cannot be pleasing to God." Many years later,
when safely behind the walls of his monastery in Bethlehem, Jerome still scornfully remembered the young widows
in Rome who used to dress in silk, wear gleaming jewels,
gold necklaces, and costly earrings made of pearls from the
Red Sea, and go about reeking of musk. Not even well-
groomed clergy were immune from Jerome's criticism.
With their curled hair and perfumed persons, they were
in his eyes nothing but vain butterflies.

Hostility turned to violence when a young nun, Blesilla
by name, died, as a result it was said of rigorous fastings
imposed upon her by Jerome. He with other monks was
set upon by the people and barely escaped alive. He was
openly ridiculed by crowds upon the street. Base accusa-

tions against him and his nuns were freely circulated. His protector, Damasus, had died and the new pope, Siricius, was no friend of the monks. Rome had become a veritable chamber of tortures for Jerome, who now decided to leave the city and take up his abode in the East where ascetics were held in greater reverence. In the summer of the year 385, with his brother Paulinus and a priest Vincentius, Jerome departed for Palestine. A few months later he was followed by a wealthy widow, Paula, accompanied by her daughter, Eustochium, and a group of faithful nuns. These pilgrims were to become the founders of the famous monastic establishment at Bethlehem begun in the year 386.

At Bethlehem, in his cell which he termed his paradise, Jerome spent the last thirty-four years of his long and industrious career. From Paula's personal resources suitable buildings had been erected, three convents for women and one for men, as well as lodgings for pilgrims. Until her death in 403, Paula seems to have borne the major part of the administrative burdens, while Jerome devoted himself to teaching the nuns and the monks, to instructing children even in classical literature, and, above all, to his study and writing. In order to perfect his knowledge of Hebrew he hired a Jewish scholar, Bar Anina, who taught him secretly at night so as to avoid arousing the hostility of the Jews. He labored continuously on the Scriptures, translating the entire Old Testament from the original Hebrew and editing more carefully his earlier revision of the Latin New Testament, a work that had been begun under the patronage of Pope Damasus. Time was found also for the composition of commentaries, the translation of significant works of earlier Greek Fathers and especially Origen, participation by letter in several theological controversies, the writ-

ing of books on a variety of subjects, and a vast correspondence with Christians in Rome and elsewhere. He taught
the monks to copy manuscripts and care for books. Shorthand writers were kept busy with his dictations, sometimes
an entire commentary being produced in a couple of nights.
Sleeplessness, it may be recalled, was a virtue with monks
in those days. Since the flesh had no rights, emaciated
bodies were the fittest tabernacles for pure souls. Before
Jerome had reached fifty he seemed to himself an old man
near death. His hair was gray and his brow wrinkled, the
loose skin hung under his chin "like the dewlaps of an ox,"
and he applied to himself the line of Virgil: "The cold
blood round my heart now hinders me." But his abused
physical frame was still to endure a quarter-century of
strenuous intellectual activity.

Although most of Jerome's significant work was a product
of his labors in the East, the outcome of his toil was the
peculiar possession of western Christendom. He wrote in
Latin and for the church in the West. His monks and nuns
at Bethlehem were mainly Christian immigrants from Italy;
Rome had migrated to Palestine without losing its identity.
The custom of making pilgrimages to the Holy Land, a
practice that figured so prominently in the later history of
European Christianity, drew its initial impulse from Jerome
and Paula. They gave to the Christian faith a new realism
by connecting it with the sacred names and sites of Palestine,
about which Jerome wrote instructive treatises. In a certain sense, he was the founder of Christian archeology.
It was as yet not so much a science for the learned as a
source of edification for the common man; pilgrimages
were, as Jerome said, "a part of the faith." The hostels
were thronged with visitors who were freely entertained,

largely at Paula's expense, in order that they might feed
their spirits upon adoration of the Savior's footsteps and
see "in all their freshness the traces of the nativity, the
cross and the passion." A personally conducted tour of
the Holy Land was, we might say, in constant operation.

It was Jerome also who awakened in the western church
its first real interest in history by making Christians more
fully conscious of the glorious past of their religion. In his
expositions of Scripture he made somewhat larger use of
geography and history than was customary in the popular
allegorical interpretation of the time. Furthermore, he
linked the past with the present by means of his historical
chronicle and his biographical writings. His accounts of the
lives of monks seem today hardly more than pious fairy
tales, but they became the model for a type of literature
that made the exemplary piety of bygone ages a source of
perpetual inspiration. Thus Jerome may be called the
Christian founder of the historical romance, a form of
writing still highly prized in many circles. His book *On
the Illustrious Men* of Christendom had a more distinctly
polemical purpose. He modeled this after a work by
Suetonius, a Roman writer of the early second century A.D.,
who had made a compendium of the most illustrious names
in the history of Latin literature. The opponents of Christianity, even in Jerome's day, were still wont to sneer at
the church for its dearth of distinguished leaders. In order
to correct this slander Jerome undertook to enlighten the
ignorance of calumniators, who "imagine that the church
has neither philosophers, orators nor teachers," by exhibiting the breadth and talents of the men who had founded,
developed, and adorned the church. His book may have
accomplished little in the way of converting critics, but it

gave to the church itself a new confidence in its noble past. Jerome was virtually the founder of patrology, an interest that was to bulk large in the future of western Catholicism.

Jerome's contribution to western monasticism is less easy to determine. He did not display the genius for organization that marked Pachomius in Egypt, or Basil in Cappadocia, or Benedict a century later in Italy. In this respect Paula was easily his superior, and her nunneries were widely imitated in future years. But his influence remained preeminent in making monasteries a center of intellectual interest where manuscripts were gathered, copied, and preserved. Similarly, as a theologian he showed almost no creative ability. He was always ready to contend valiantly for orthodoxy and, when his own position was called in question, did not hesitate to quarrel with bosom friends like Rufinus, or to condemn the views of Origen, to whom he probably owed a larger intellectual obligation than to any other man of the ancient church. But it was Origen's factual knowledge, rather than the aggressiveness of his creative thinking, that registered with Jerome. In a moment of ingenuous disloyalty he writes: "I laud the exegesis of Origen and not his doctrine, his genius and not his faith, the scholar and not the propagandist."

Jerome was at his best as a translator of Scripture. In this field he had stout convictions which he was prepared to defend against all critics. This was the field in which he made his most valuable and permanent contribution to the church. While still in Rome he had undertaken, at the urging of Damasus, a revision of the Latin New Testament then in general use in Italy. He sought as far as possible to retain the language of a text held sacred because of its familiarity. But when he brought together various Latin versions, comparing them with the original Greek, he found it necessary to make a number of changes. It was inevitable that popular sentiment should protest, but Jerome's conscience was clear and he had no patience with critics. He called them "little men" who were only "two-legged asses." While enjoying the approval of the pope, he felt no need to be conciliatory.

The work at Rome had been only preliminary to the larger task of making an entirely new rendering of the Old Testament on the basis of the original Hebrew. He spent some fourteen years on this enterprise at Bethlehem, where he produced his famous Latin Bible now commonly known as the Vulgate, which, with some slight revisions, still remains the authentic text of the Roman Catholic Church. But at the outset it was almost universally condemned. No churchmen of the West knew any Hebrew, and those who prided themselves on a knowledge of Greek could not endure to have the Septuagint, the Bible that had been taken over from the Greek-speaking Jews of the Dispersion, set aside. This version, heretofore used by all the great leaders of the church, had become sacred in its own right. When Jerome deviated from its familiar language, in the interest of fidelity to the original Hebrew, he seemed to be giving the lie to the ancient worthies and to be guilty of sacrilege. Even the great Augustine of North Africa passionately accused Jerome of perverting Scripture. Our modern translators, who venture to change the familiar language of the revered King James version, know well how bitterly the public can resent any tampering with traditional phrases in the interest of more accurate renderings.

Jerome did not live to see his monumental labor and genuine scholarship vindicated. But time was to prove kind to his memory. Not only did his translation win general acceptance in the West, but its vocabulary entered largely into the fabric of the church's theology and liturgy, and through these channels flowed abundantly into the making of the romance languages and literatures of the European peoples.

AUGUSTINE

Augustine, Jerome's younger contemporary, was predominantly a man of the West. He was born at Tagaste on November 13, 354, and died at Hippo Regius on August 28, 430. Except for a year's residence in Rome and three years in Milan, he spent his entire life in North Africa. He was purely a product of Latin culture. He was wholly ignorant of Hebrew, none too familiar with Greek, and did not take the trouble to visit the eastern patriarchates, monasteries or sacred places. Augustine was no satellite reflecting only borrowed light; he shone by his own brilliancy as the creator of Roman Catholic theology. In fact he was the first Christian thinker to elaborate a comprehensive and well-rounded doctrinal system.

It is very true that the church had formulated a substantial body of theological concepts long before the time of Augustine. Specific beliefs had characterized Christianity from the start. While even Paul had been no mean theologian, succeeding centuries produced many individuals who distinguished themselves in the field of Christian doctrine. By the close of the second century traditional Christian teaching had been epitomized in a form practically identical with the statement now commonly known as the Apostles' Creed. In the early third century, Origen had written his *First Principles* and a hundred years later the

Council of Nicæa had issued an authoritative declaration on the position of Christ in the Godhead. Still later, synods and councils debated and legislated on various problems of dogma. But a thoroughly comprehensive statement had not yet been composed.

The finished theologian must have an answer for every possible question about faith and conduct as these concern religious people. He must define the nature, character, and activities of God and of his associated divine beings—Christ, the Holy Spirit and the angels. The origin, meaning, and future of the world have to be determined. How and why man was created, the constituent elements in his being, the rôle he is to play in history, the way in which the divine will is made known to him, his duties toward God and toward other men, and his ultimate destiny, must be expounded. Also the problem of evil has to be solved—how evil originated, its modes of operation in the individual and in the universe, how it can be resisted, and the manner of effecting its overthrow. The theologian must know well the devil and all his works. The church, too, has to be fully explained—how it arose, what its nature is, the significance of its rites, its proper organization and government, and its functions in society and in cosmic history. Such is the all-inclusive task of the accomplished theologian.

Various forces shape every man's theological opinions, but in the case of Augustine the genetic factors were exceptionally complex. His emotional and intellectual make-up intensified his feelings to an unusually high degree and made the quest for truth seem to him almost a life-and-death struggle. His keen social sensitivity bred in him a consciousness of dependence that rendered existence intolerable apart from association with friends. The solitary life of meditation was unattractive to a man of his temper, and when he did retire for quiet thought he took along congenial companions to aid and share in the search for the deep things of the spirit. This responsiveness to environment left its mark upon his life from the cradle to the grave. Augustine had occasion to lament the errors into which he had been led by evil companions in his youth, and this same trait in his personality caused him to place divine friendship at the core of his theological thinking, a sentiment aptly expressed in his famous confession to God: "Thou hast made us for Thyself and our heart is restless until it finds repose in Thee."

At the same time Augustine was possessed of a remarkably alert and creative mind that exercised itself upon a wide range of individual and social contacts. Religion was a theme that had been pressed upon his attention in earliest childhood by his Christian mother, Monica. The fact that his father, Patricius, was a pagan, probably only heightened the boy's religious consciousness. But the atmosphere of the home seems not to have been a contentious one, and both parents cherished high hopes for the future career of their son. They planned to give him the best education afforded by the times, although they were not themselves persons of wealth, his father being "only a poor freeman." Augustine received an elementary training in his native place, Tagaste, a small inland town of North Africa, some fifty miles south of Hippo Regius. Later he was sent to Madaura, a larger town to the south of Tagaste, to pursue further study. He returned home in the summer of the year 369, when his father immediately undertook to assemble the necessary funds to send his son to school at Carthage. Augustine was now in his sixteenth year.

In Tagaste Augustine now had a few months of idleness during which, he says, "the briers of unclean desires grew rank over my head." He had not been a studious youth. At least, so we must infer, if he has not misrepresented himself. He had acquired a knowledge of reading, writing, and arithmetic under the lash; otherwise he would have learned nothing. Greek he hated, and failed to gain any mastery of the language. But his curiosity was insatiable, while his lively imagination reveled in passages from the poets. Virgil's account of the wanderings of Æneas so delighted him that he shed copious tears over the story of Dido self-slain for love of her hero. In later years he lamented the misspent hours when beautiful words and tender sentiments had drawn him into the "hellish torrent" of Latin poetry where his soul had been soiled by the empty and vile thoughts of paganism. Yet even after he had turned a deaf ear to all heathen vanities, he gratefully recognized the debt he owed to an educational discipline that had skilled him "in rich and adorned and well-ordered discourse."

Although Augustine's father had now become a catechumen, he still wished to give his son further training in preparation for a rhetorical profession. But the father suddenly died. However, a wealthy citizen of Tagaste came to the aid of the family, and Augustine went to Carthage for two years of study. There he lived under the sway of impulse, plunged in "a cauldron of unholy loves"—love of lust, love of the theater, love of vagrant liberty, and love of eloquent discourse. He quite neglected serious thoughts until one day when he was nineteen years of age he came upon a work of Cicero called the *Hortensius*, a dialogue on philosophy. This book, Augustine says, altered his whole

future activity by inspiring him to undertake the search for
true knowledge.   He had read the book to "sharpen" his
tongue, but its contents had filled him with a "burning desire for an immortality of wisdom."   As he looked back
upon the event from the vantage-ground of later years he
perceived that it had been the turning point at which he
began to direct his way toward God.

The *Hortensius* is no longer extant, but Augustine has
cited several paragraphs that lodged in his memory.   These
indicate that he had been much impressed by passages ex-
horting the thoughtful person to rise above mere mundane
concerns to the contemplation of the universe and the destiny of man's immortal spirit.   One quotation seems to have
struck Augustine with peculiar force: "If, as ancient philosophers thought—and these too the greatest and by far the
most celebrated—we have souls eternal and divine, then we
must needs think that the more these shall have always kept
in their own proper course, that is, in reason and research,
the less they shall have mixed and entangled themselves in
the vices and errors of men and the more easily will they
ascend and return to heaven."

Like an infant learning to walk, Augustine's initial footsteps along his new path were faltering and irregular.   His
heart, now set on acquiring wisdom, was sufficiently under
the influence of a Christian heritage to recognize that
knowledge of God was the ultimate goal of its quest.   But
how was God to be found?   The Catholic church to which
Augustine's mother belonged had a ready answer: Accept
the authoritative teachings of Scripture.   But when Augustine read these books in the old Latin translation then current in North Africa they offended his literary taste; they
seemed to him "unworthy to be compared to the stateliness

of Tully (Cicero)." Also there were other features unacceptable to the questioning mind of the intelligent youth, unwilling to receive as ultimate truth statements that he could not justify by rational processes. He was not yet ready to submit himself blindly to the authority of either an ecclesiastical institution or a sacred book.

At this time in North Africa there was another Christian denomination with a considerable following, known as the Manicheans. These congregations stood for "modernism." Having inherited a large element of the older Gnostic skepticism as to the literal validity of the Old Testament, they encouraged their adherents to measure truth by the test of rationality. Faith was not to be imposed upon one by an ecclesiastical fiat but was to be perceived by the apprehending mind in response to the dictates of logic. These religionists claimed to represent the true and original Christianity. This presentation appealed to Augustine and he joined the Manicheans as a "hearer," maintaining the attachment for the next nine years.

In the year 374, Augustine returned to Tagaste where he became a teacher of rhetoric. He was not legally married, but while a student in Carthage, following a respectable Roman custom of the time, he had acquired a concubine who had borne him a son named Adeodatus. The relationship was essentially that of wedlock and was so regarded by Augustine—a kind of "companionate marriage," to use a modern phrase. But other friendships were richer in meaning for him. His love for his mother was deep and abiding, although the two had little in common within the intellectual sphere. She was so scandalized and distressed by his adhesion to the Manichean church that on his return to Tagaste she refused to share her home with him. But his old benefactor, Romanianus, received Augustine into his own household, making him tutor to his son Licentius. A strong attachment was formed with other friends who, under the influence of the young teacher, were induced to join the Manicheans. One of these companions, whose name is unrecorded, suddenly fell ill and died. This loss seemed to the sensitive Augustine more than he could bear. His grief was so intense that he could no longer endure the familiar sights in Tagaste that constantly suggested his deceased friend and brought on fresh fits of violent weeping whenever he saw anything that revived old memories. Describing his agony he tells us that "only tears were sweet to me, for they succeeded my friend in the dearest of my affections."

In order to shake off his sorrow Augustine moved to Carthage. He was now about twenty-three years of age and for the next eight years he maintained himself as a teacher of rhetoric in the city where he had previously been a student. He retained his attachment to the Manichean church, but his inquiring mind was leading him deeper and deeper into doubts as to the validity of certain Manichean doctrines. An opportunity for a conference with one of the most learned bishops of this communion, Faustus, who was on a visit to Carthage, only increased Augustine's skepticism. The chief point at issue seems to have been the origin of evil. This was not, at least for Augustine, a purely academic issue. He was so thoroughly dominated by his emotions that he felt keenly the need to locate the source of those good and evil impulses that waged ceaseless warfare within his being. Evil in particular was the enemy whose secret he wished to discover.

The Manicheans had their own answer. Evil, they said,

was a material rather than a spiritual thing. The wickedness of the scorpion was in its sting; remove the physical poison and the evil disappeared. But what Augustine really wanted to know was why scorpions existed at all. On the other hand, the Manicheans were really pragmatists; their Christianity was a way of acting rather than a system of dogma. While Augustine was not averse to the pursuit of virtue, he demanded a philosophical explanation to support conduct. Faustus gave him rules when he asked for theories—gave him ethics when he sought theology, gave him practical instruction instead of speculative wisdom. "Modernist" that he was, Faustus seems to have deplored the futility of theological theory, which was the quest most intriguing to the inquisitive Augustine. The urbanity of Faustus and the plausibility of his discourse seemed only a beautiful but empty cup offered to one athirst for a draft of satisfying "truth."

Augustine's dissatisfaction did not at once become fully evident even to himself. But his confidence in Manichean teaching was seriously shaken. In the autumn of 383 he again changed his residence, this time moving to Rome to follow his profession. Students at Carthage had been too boisterous for his tastes, but he soon discovered that those of Rome were both fickle and dishonest. The entire group would suddenly abandon one teacher to take up with another before paying their fees to the former. When the people of Milan asked the Roman prefect, Symmachus, to recommend a rhetorician to them, Augustine's name was presented and he transferred to Milan in the year 384. There, captivated by the preaching of Ambrose, Augustine took a place among the catechumens in the Catholic church. His mind was not yet fully made up as to the future; his new line of action was a temporary procedure to mark time, as he says, "till something certain should dawn upon me, whither I might steer my course."

During his period of indecision Augustine cast about for new means by which to bring his mind to rest. In Rome he had resided with a Manichean "hearer" and was still counted, no doubt, as a member of that group, but his discontent with its dogmas was increasing. He began, in fact, to question the possibility of the human mind's ability to arrive at final truth. He now felt a strong leaning toward the school of philosophy known as the "Academics." They held that absolute certainty was unattainable; objective appearances were often deceptive and the physical senses could not always be trusted. Logic also might lead one astray if rational processes dealt with uncertain data, and religion seemed especially prone to accept unproved or undemonstrable postulates. Even in matters of morals, how could one always be sure of one's way?

Doubt was a state of mind utterly uncongenial to Augustine's temperament; he could not long remain in a state of suspense. But where was final truth to be found? He had lost confidence in Manichean pragmatism, but Academic skepticism gave him no peace. Only one of two possible courses remained open. Either he might surrender his independence of thinking to the scripturally authenticated dogmas of the Catholic church, or he might explore the possibilities of still another philosophical school whose founders' writings had recently been translated from Greek into Latin by Victorinus, the most celebrated rhetorician at Rome in Augustine's day. For the moment, he chose the latter alternative. Reading the Neoplatonic books he found a large measure of satisfaction in yielding to their teachings.

In a world where the complexities of life and the break-down of external authorities in society forced the competent individual to fall back on his own resources, other sensitive spirits had, like Augustine, been impelled to turn away from external phenomena to the inner self for satisfaction. Critical study of objective data, and logical reasoning therefrom, were not convenient tools for use in this situation. Of much greater service were a cultivation of elevated feeling and a resort to the mysterious. These were the chosen implements of the Neoplatonic philosopher. The material world and the physical senses played a relatively insignificant rôle in his quest for wisdom. On the contrary, he thought that the truth on which he could rely with greatest confidence was simply the consciousness of his own existence. Similarly, the ultimate truth of the universe was the supreme and all-embracing principle of pure Being, the divine Absolute, the perfect Unity, the supreme Good. He was truly wise who attained a state of mind that felt itself one with "the One," that adored and thirsted for and loved above all else the Supreme Unity, whence everything that is lovable, beautiful and truthful has its source.

No one who has read a half-dozen pages of Augustine's *Confessions*, which apart from the Bible is probably the best known book that has come down to us from the ancient church, will need to be reminded of Neoplatonism's strong and enduring influence upon the Christianity of Augustine. His conversion to Neoplatonic philosophy was a long step in the direction of a return to the Catholic church of his childhood. But he did not act precipitously, nor does he seem to have sought formal ecclesiastical guidance from Ambrose, whose preaching he greatly admired. But a priest, Simplicianus, gave him valuable assistance. Also his mother had followed him to Italy, and in Milan a choice coterie of friends was wont to assemble in private where together they thought through their problems. Augustine was led to a new regard for Scripture, the difficulties that had formerly troubled him being greatly relieved by the figurative meanings expounded in Ambrose's sermons. Then, also, news came to Augustine that the rhetorician Victorinus had accepted Christianity. If this man of exquisite literary taste could bow to the authority of the Scriptures, Augustine may have reasoned that a similar submission on his part would not be unbecoming.

At this time another determining influence—one might call it a mere accident—entered into Augustine's life. An African officer, Pontitianus, when on a visit to Milan told Augustine about Antony, an Egyptian anchorite, the story of whose life of self-denial Athanasius had carried to the West. Pontitianus, who had heard it at Trier in Gaul, had been much impressed, as was Augustine also by the narrative and by Pontitianus' testimony to its effect on his own life. The spirit of monasticism was in the air, but heretofore it had not arrested the attention of Augustine. Until he got the news from his visitor he did not know that the revered Ambrose had under his fostering care a monastery "full of good brethren" outside the walls of Milan. Augustine had been debating for some time as to his own future procedure. He was bent on acquiring philosophical wisdom, but was not certain that he wished to abandon the hope of worldly honors and deny himself the satisfaction of normal physical appetites. He had dismissed his concubine only to provide himself with another, whom he intended also to give up when he could find a marriageable woman of means whose income would enable him to pursue the unremunerative life of a philosopher—a Christian philosopher, of course, as he understood that profession.

The conversation with Pontitianus, supplementing the reading of the Pauline epistles on which Augustine had recently been engaged, opened up afresh the whole question of his future. Ought he not at once to renounce outright all worldly ambitions and give himself over completely to a life of continence and monastic simplicity? This was the state of mind that prefaced the famous incident in the garden, commonly known as Augustine's "conversion." While reclining alone under a tree in meditation it seemed as if he heard the voice of a child chanting, "Take up and read, take up and read" (*Tolle lege, tolle lege*). He recalled how Antony had suddenly changed his mode of life when one day there fell upon his ears on entering a church: "Go sell all that you have and give to the poor." Augustine rushed into the house where his friend Alypius was sitting and, seizing the book containing Paul's epistles, he opened it at random to find his eye resting on the passage where Paul admonished the Romans to "put on the Lord Jesus Christ and make not provision for the flesh to fulfil the lusts thereof." The message seemed to be a direct communication from Heaven.

Thus Augustine had at last solved his lifelong quest for certainty. Ultimate wisdom was to be found in Scripture. He had been converted—converted to the authority of the Bible rather than to the creed or to the government of the Catholic church. He still had a long way to go before attaining his majority, so to speak, as a theologian and an ecclesiastic. It was now the summer of the year 386. The next month, at the end of the summer term, he resigned his professorship on the excuse of ill health and retired with his mother and a select group of companions to a friend's country house not far from Milan. There the time was spent in devotion, meditation and conference. Ambrose had advised them to read the prophecies of Isaiah, evidently aiming to strengthen their faith in Christ's fulfilment of Old Testament predictions, but Augustine found Isaiah wearisome and substituted the Psalms. The vivid portrayal of a religious man's feelings, as he sank to the depths and rose to the heights, was better suited to Augustine's temperament. He also read again, this time aloud to his companions, Cicero's *Hortensius*, which they found impressive and stimulating. They engaged in discussion, as did Cicero and his friends, with a stenographer present to record their conversation. The transcriptions were revised by Augustine, three books being thus composed during the winter: *Against the Academies*, *On the Blessed Life*, and *On the Order of the Universe*. Strangely enough, they betray nothing of the high emotionalism and torment of spirit that Augustine in later years, when writing his *Confessions*, connected with the period of his "conversion." Perhaps he was now living in the calm that followed the storm.

In the spring of 387, Augustine returned to Milan and at Easter received baptism, along with his friend Alypius and his son Adeodatus, who was now nearly fifteen years of age. Preparations were made at once for the return to Africa. At Ostia, the seaport of Rome, Monica died. The account of her death and burial is one of the most touching passages in Augustine's *Confessions*. Monica's parting injunction had been, "Lay this body anywhere; let not care for it concern you." The burial rites were therefore simple and the mourners were self-controlled, as befitted those who laid away their beloved dead in the full hope of the Christian resurrection. But on returning from the grave Augustine gave way to a flood of tears which he thought not improper for the son of a mother now "dead to my eyes, who for many years had wept for me."

Returning to Africa, Augustine settled at Tagaste. He disposed of his small inheritance and contributed the proceeds to the poor. He and his companions devoted themselves to study and writing. Adeodatus, who gave promise of remarkable ability, died in his seventeenth year. In 391 A.D., Augustine visited Hippo Regius on a mission of mercy, and the aged bishop Valerius, desiring an efficient helper, ordained him to the priesthood. Four years later, when the bishop died, Augustine was appointed his successor and continued to occupy this position of ecclesiastical responsibility for the next thirty-five years.

The episcopal office imposed upon Augustine many new duties that compelled him to reshape and expand his theology. Heretofore he had been preëminently an individualist, but now he became the defender and interpreter of an institution. He never lost his zest for meditation and interpretative thinking, but the forces that impinged upon him in those trying times furnished ample incentive for the development of that system of theological thought that has rendered him famous. The Manicheans, still numerous and aggressive, had to be vigorously refuted. In resisting them Augustine elaborated his teaching on the validity of Scriptural revelation and reasserted his doctrine of evil, as arising in man's will to stray from God rather than in any material substance. God is the only true reality—a Neoplatonic conception—whose will is so supreme that even his grace is irresistible. He foreknows everything and therefore predestines man for salvation or damnation. To say that this divine foreordination is unjust to man, ignores the fact that he merits nothing but condemnation; if some men obtain salvation because God has elected them to this privilege, that is to be credited to his divine love and wisdom. Absolute submission to Deity is the only road to truth; the exercise of human reason advocated by the Manicheans is utter vanity.

The Donatist denomination, that had caused offense to Constantine, was still thriving in Africa and impelled Augustine to develop his doctrines about the nature of the church and its sacraments. He had no sympathy with the belligerent puritanism of the Donatists. A church established by God and mediating salvation through its sacraments could not have its efficacy conditioned or its authority limited by the defects of its human clergy. The visible church might include unworthy persons, but the invisible church was the ultimate reality, supreme in its authority, universal in its scope, and infallible in its decrees. Even bishops and councils might on occasion err, but the true church was God's Kingdom already set up on earth, the authentic teacher of mankind, destined for supremacy over all peoples and nations. Coercion by the state was not out of place when used to instil "wholesome fear" into persons prone to join protesting Christian sects.

In Augustine's theology, the counterpart of God's sufficiency in all things was natural man's utter perversity, helplessness, and dependence upon divine love and grace for everything that he is or ever hopes to be. He could do nothing for himself. While he had free will to pursue evil, he was not of himself able to choose God. Until his natural will-power had been reinforced by Deity—the help that Augustine calls "grace"—man could not turn to God nor could human effort, in itself, accomplish any saving work. God "predestined" the number of the elect, he insured the "perseverance of the saints," his "prevenient grace" alone could awaken saving faith in men and stimulate their wills to action. These notions were reaffirmed and further developed by Augustine in conflict with a new sect of Christians that appeared in Africa soon after the opening of the fifth century. Its founder was the monk Pelagius, perhaps a native of Britain, who came to Rome about the year 400, and who stressed man's responsibility for working out his own salvation, even if with fear and trembling. Thus arose what we might call a "humanist" church, with which Augustine had to deal.

The sack of Rome by Alaric in the year 410 drove many of the Pelagians to Africa. They emphasized human effort as a corrective for the laxity in daily living evident in the case of many church members. The Pelagians would make more of morals, if not less of theology. Every person was directly accountable to God for the exercise of a free will that chose good or evil as it liked. Each man's sin was his own rather than an inheritance from Adam. The first man had fallen, as did his descendants, by yielding to temptation; the responsibility always rested with the individual. Divine grace operated, not as compulsion but as helpful goodness, strengthening and stimulating men toward worthy moral and spiritual attainments. The number of the saved was not predetermined; everyone was free to seek and obtain such a measure of salvation as his efforts deserved. All of these views were resisted by Augustine, who reiterated his counter opinions regarding the total depravity of man, the utter worthlessness of any attempt to help himself out of his condition, the absoluteness of the divine will in electing men to salvation and insuring their perseverance, and like notions issuing from that extreme contrast between God and man so confidently preached by Augustine and revived in recent times by Karl Barth.

Augustine did not face the crucial political problems that engaged the attention of Ambrose, but he was called upon to defend the church against the popular charge that it was to blame for the distresses into which the state had fallen. Christian apologists had proclaimed for centuries that their God alone was able to insure the safety of the state. But within two decades after Christianity had been made the only legal religion of the Roman Empire, the invading Goths under Alaric's leadership had captured and plundered "eternal" Rome. When Jerome in Bethlehem heard this astounding news it seemed to him that the light of the world had been extinguished. The Empire had been decapitated; the whole world had perished in one city. Augustine was still nearer to the scene of the calamity and Africa was filled with refugees from Italy. The alert mind of Augustine undertook an interpretation of the situation. The result was his exposition of political theory and his philosophy of history contained in a monumental work entitled the *City of God*, a book that was to exert a mighty influence in later times when the church in Europe was struggling to make all princes bow to its will.

When Augustine died at Hippo Regius the Vandals were before its walls. Their triumph was already assured. The light of Christianity in North Africa was on the verge of extinction. It flickered up faintly into new brightness when Justinian's armies overthrew the Vandal power in the next century, and then was snuffed out completely by the Moslem conquest a century later. But Augustine's memory could not perish. He had labored for the church universal and the brilliancy of his work continued to shine with undimmed splendor upon western Christendom throughout subsequent years. His fertile mind, ranging over a vast expanse of interests, produced a system of theology that was long to reign as "Queen of the Sciences." In its main features, as well as in many of its details, it still dominates the thinking of Roman Catholicism and permeates extensive areas of Protestantism.

CHAPTER VII

STATESMEN OF WESTERN CHRISTENDOM

By the middle of the fifth century society in the western half of the Roman world was trembling on the brink of chaos. The imperial administration had almost completely collapsed. Its armies, largely recruited from barbarian mercenaries and frequently officered by men of foreign birth, had failed to maintain the territorial integrity of the Empire. Britain had been abandoned, the Vandals had possessed themselves of North Africa, the Visigoths had occupied Spain and southern Gaul, the Burgundians had settled in the upper regions of the Rhine and the Rhône, from the North the Franks were pressing into central Gaul, and the Ostrogoths were menacing Italy. On all sides evidences of decadence were apparent.

In this period of political decline western emperors remained the nominal rulers, but the power of the "eternal" city on the Tiber had become an empty tradition. The senate, it is true, still survived, and many aristocratic families continued to reside in Rome. They were, however, virtually helpless. Aggressive emperors in the earlier times had curtailed the authority of the senate until it had become a pale shadow of its former self and was quite unequal to the task of leading effectively in the rehabilitation of the distressed social order. The imperial court had moved first to Milan and then to Ravenna, where it impotently existed in comparative safety behind the impenetrable marshes that

188

enveloped the city on its landward side. No efficient administrators emerged from this royal sanctuary. Constantinople still dominated the East, but its emperors were usually inspired by selfish or predatory motives when they concerned themselves with the problems of the West.

Whither could the people of Italy look for help? Society needed leaders who possessed the old Roman talent for government, who had a genius for administration, and who could restore some sort of unity amid the flood of disintegrating forces that were inundating the land. The church at Rome came to the rescue. There was no longer any generally powerful secular arm whose strength seriously menaced the will of bishops, as in the days of Ambrose; nor could the state, whose favor was still courted, if not indeed commanded, serve adequately the world-wide needs of a universal Christendom. The church was compelled to produce its own statesmen. They worked from within the institution and through its agencies toward the establishment of a social order sponsored and controlled by ecclesiastical authority. This new trend in western Europe is seen conspicuously in the activities of Leo the Great, Benedict of Nursia and Gregory the Great.

Leo the Great

Leo was born during the closing years of the fourth century, perhaps in Rome, although one tradition makes him a native of Tuscany. The nature of his education is known to us only by inference, but it was typically Roman, as were his temperament and interests. Above all else, he was a churchman. Unlike Jerome and Augustine, he showed no fondness for classical literature, although he possessed a good working knowledge of the Latin language. His sermons and letters were effectively phrased and his ideas clearly stated, yet without any attempt at formal elegance or any flair for speculative reasoning. His attention was centered on practical values. Regularity, official control, the subordination of individualism in the interests of uniformity, and reverence for authority were as prominent in his mentality as they had been in the psychology of the most competent early Roman emperors.

Even in his youth Leo seems to have been an important personage in the Roman church. Perhaps he was the young acolyte who in the year 418 carried a letter from Pope Zosimus to Carthage urging action against the Pelagians. In the days of Pope Celestine (422-432 A.D.) Leo was an archdeacon. At his solicitation John Cassian, a notable monastic leader from the East who had migrated to southern Gaul, wrote a treatise on the incarnation to counteract the teachings of Nestorius, the patriarch of Constantinople whom the Council of Ephesus condemned in the year 431 because he had so strongly insisted on differentiating between the divine and the human natures in Jesus that he protested against applying to Mary the epithet "Theotokos," meaning "one giving birth to God," "Mother of God." Cassian, in the preface to his work, called Leo the "ornament of the Roman church and of the divine ministry." At this time the bishop of Alexandria also bore witness to Leo's prominence by seeking from him, rather than from the Pope, support for the policy of the Alexandrian church in dealing with certain problems of ecclesiastical order in Palestine.

Under Pope Sixtus III (432-440 A.D.) Leo continued to be alert and powerful in both church and state. In the year 439 he was sent by the western emperor, Valentinian III, to negotiate a reconciliation between Ætius and Albinus, two rival Roman generals in Gaul. The quarrel can hardly have been occasioned by religious issues, and the choice of Leo as the imperial agent to compose the differences places him among the outstanding men of Italy even before he became bishop of Rome. He was still, or was again, in Gaul when Sixtus died in the summer of 440. Immediately Leo was popularly acclaimed pope and entered upon his new duties late in September. For over two decades he continued in office, displaying a capacity for ecclesiastical generalship and an imperial consciousness such as had never before been manifested by any Roman pontiff.

Leo had a lofty conception of his new functions. In his brief inaugural address he made plain his sense of responsibility not only to the local community but to the church at large. A local bishop was a shepherd of his own flock, while the bishop of Rome, being Peter's successor, was the shepherd of all congregations. Everything that had to do with the universal church and all its members in every part of the world—discipline, clerical ordinations, parish administration, maintenance of correct doctrine, conciliar decisions, relations with secular authorities—was a care for the bishop of bishops. In no spirit of arrogance, but with a deep feeling of obligation to discharge faithfully his God-imposed task, Leo took up the duties of his office. Since the whole world had access to the blessed see of Peter, his successor must carry out the Lord's command enjoining upon the prince of the apostles a love of the brethren. Leo would "serve rather than command," but since his commission was from Heaven, obedience on the part of those to whom he ministered was an indispensable virtue.

Leo was determined to make the power of the church,

radiating from Rome as the center of its authority, dominant in the crumbling Roman Empire. His dealings with rulers—western and eastern emperors, and barbarian princes—sometimes caused him anxious moments. In general, however, the authorities of the court at Ravenna stood ready to do his bidding. Constantinople was less subservient but put in his way no serious obstacles, except in the case of the memorable twenty-eighth canon of the Council of Chalcedon (451 A.D.) which gave to "the most holy church of Constantinople, or New Rome" an equality with old Rome that was highly displeasing to Leo. This action placed the churches of Thrace, Pontus and Asia under the absolute jurisdiction of the patriarch of Constantinople, thus making him supreme in the East and wholly independent of the bishop of Rome. This ruling was justified on the ground that the imperial capital had been moved to Constantinople. Although western emperors now resided in Ravenna, this city was unable to command the respect of either church or state. Fortunately for Leo the conflict was one of words, not of armies, and his vigorous protest, supplemented by the influence he exerted in connection with the doctrinal disputes that agitated the East, won him at least a moral triumph. While a man of Leo's power occupied the Roman see, its prestige remained supreme.

At two crises in his lifetime Leo encountered barbarian princes. The army of the fierce Attila, king of the Huns, sweeping like a scourge across the northern parts of the Empire, moved upon Rome in the year 452. There being no Roman soldiers to resist the invader, the devastation of the city seemed imminent. Then Leo came to the aid of the terrified people. Accompanied by two men of high rank, he went forth to negotiate with the enemy.   Legend has so overlaid the incident with pious ornamentation that, in the absence of any specific reference to it by Leo himself, the historical facts are no longer recoverable.   We only know that, for some obscure reason, Attila turned back, led his army home to recruit new forces for an attack on the eastern Empire, and died of hemorrhage while celebrating his wedding feast the following year.

Leo's appeal to Gaiseric, the Vandal king from North Africa who attacked Rome in the year 455, was less successful.   The bishop has been given the credit for persuading the conquerors to refrain from slaughter of the people and from setting fire to the buildings.   Nevertheless, for two weeks the Vandals plundered the city of such treasures as had escaped the ravages of the Visigoths under Alaric in 410.   An enormous amount of spoils was loaded on to the ships, along with many prisoners, and carried away to Africa.   Yet the fact that the churches had suffered less than other public buildings seemed to indicate God's care for his people.   The departure of the Vandals became an annual day of thanksgiving on which Leo exhorted the people to recall with gratitude their deliverance.   The disaster had been a punishment for their sins, but divine pity had yielded to the pleadings of the "benevolent Peter and all the saints."

Leo was untiring in his efforts to restore and establish on firmer foundations the unity of Christendom, in both doctrine and government, under the aegis of Rome.   This was his greatest and most enduring gift to the western church. He had toiled at the task before he became bishop, and throughout his episcopal administration he remained devoted to this ideal.

Against the Manicheans he waged bitter warfare. Following the Vandal invasion of Africa large numbers of them had fled to Italy. They were found to be secretly organizing at Rome as early as the year 439. Four years later Leo launched a formidable attack against the sectaries. In public assemblies they were scathingly arraigned, their books were gathered and burned, their teachers and church officials were arrested, and the emperor Valentinian III was induced to issue an edict supporting the church in its holy war against heretics. Leo addressed a forceful letter to the bishops throughout Italy warning them to be on guard and reminding them that the Christian emperor had authorized public judges to banish "into perpetual exile" Manicheans who refused to recant.

Pelagians were also suspected. They, too, had left Africa to escape the Vandals and seek a more congenial home in Italy. There they attached themselves to the Catholic congregations, participating in the rites of worship without openly renouncing their doubts about the doctrine of total depravity and prevenient grace as preached by Augustine. This easy-going conduct could not be tolerated by Leo. Persons suspected of heresy ought not to be received into communion until they had made a definite retraction of their errors. Even when this had been done they needed still to be watched lest some of their former perversities should crop out again, and especial care had to be taken in the event that they sought clerical advancement.

Leo's zeal for orthodoxy was not confined to Italy. He was quite ready to attempt the suppression of the Priscillianists in Spain. Their founder, a man of learning and piety, had suffered martyrdom for his faith in a Catholic persecution of his church late in the fourth century. But the movement had survived. Its tenets involved features of Gnostic and Manichean teaching regarding the inadequacy of the Old Testament as a body of Christian revelation and the freedom of Christ from contact with evil matter. More serious was their unwillingness to submit to the authority of the Catholic church. In Leo's day a local Spanish bishop circulated letters against them and wrote to the bishop of Rome for help. Leo was only too ready to comply with this request. He replied, presenting a detailed refutation of alleged Priscillianist errors, and advised the calling of a council. But the unsettled state of government in Spain made impossible any final settlement of the difficulties, even with Leo's intervention.

In the East Leo's enterprises came out more successfully, although they suffered some temporarily disheartening reverses. The eastern churches were involved in a doctrinal controversy arising out of the Nestorian dispute. Jealous patriarchs, in their conflicts with one another, appealed to Leo for assistance. Convinced that Rome was divinely empowered to dictate correct faith to the church universal, he gladly availed himself of the opportunity to speak. It was in this connection that he composed what is perhaps his best known theological treatise, the *Tome*. It was written in the year 449 in the form of a letter addressed to Flavian, patriarch of Constantinople. In taking this action Leo antagonized the patriarch of Alexandria, who was hostile to Flavian. But Alexandrian influence was for the moment in the ascendancy at the imperial court, which called a synod at Ephesus where Flavian was deposed and Leo's advice was ignored—a "robber" synod as Leo dubbed it.

Then, suddenly, the emperor died, and political sentiment at Constantinople changed. The new ruler summoned a council at Chalcedon, which met in the year 451 and formulated its theological position in harmony with the *Tome* of Leo. When the document was read the assembled dignitaries exclaimed, "Peter has spoken by the mouth of Leo." It was a proud day for the Roman bishop, whose joy was marred somewhat by the inclusion of the twenty-eighth canon mentioned above. While this canon limited Leo's administrative supremacy, his right to dictate in matters of theology remained unimpaired. The outcome must also have relieved considerably his disappointment over his failure to persuade the eastern ruler that the synod should have been held in Italy, which he had insisted was the proper place for an ecumenical council.

In the West the administrative autonomy of Rome was newly affirmed by Leo. Pope Zosimus (417-418 A.D.) had conceded to the bishop of Arles supremacy over the churches in Gaul. This Leo virtually repudiated when an occasion arose for him to interfere. He humiliated Hilary, the powerful metropolitan of Arles, and secured from Valentinian III in the year 445 the promulgation of a decree enacting "that not only the bishops of Gaul, but those of the other provinces, shall attempt nothing contrary to ancient custom without the authority of the venerable father of the Eternal City. Whatever shall be sanctioned by the Apostolic See shall be law to them and to everyone else." Henceforth, opposition to the rulings of Leo rendered the offender guilty of treason.

Leo was both good and great, a man of high character, masterly purpose and consecrated ambition, who had answered the call of the hour for a leader to steady the trembling structure of the disrupted social order in the western Mediterranean lands. With a strong hand he exercised over the actions and thinking of his contemporaries a supervision which he conscientiously believed had been delegated to him by Heaven. His domain was the entire Christian world and his power was from God, mediated through Christ, Peter, and the divinely ordained Roman see. In its bishop the transcendent authority of the blessed Peter was still resident. Political dominion, since it rested on a human basis, was inferior to the rule of the church built "on the rock which the Lord had laid as a foundation." Swayed by this conviction, Leo sought to enforce his will throughout Italy and beyond into such parts of North Africa as had not fallen to the Vandals, and into Spain, Gaul, Egypt, Palestine, Asia Minor, and the Balkan peninsula to the very gates of Constantinople. It is little wonder that he has been called the "founder of the medieval papacy."

BENEDICT OF NURSIA

Some twenty years after the death of Leo (461 A.D.) Benedict was born. His native place was Nursia, a municipality of Umbria lying about eighty miles north of Rome. As the son of a wealthy family, he was sent to Rome to finish his education. The pious youth was ill at ease in unfamiliar surroundings, while the vices of the city shocked his moral sensibilities. To add to his distress, he fell in love with a Roman lady. But, yearning for sainthood, he suddenly decided to withdraw secretly, to abandon his studies, and to adopt the life of a hermit. Thus he hoped to realize his supreme ambition "to please God alone." His quest for a place of solitude took him eastward through the hills of Latium to the ruins of a palace of Nero at Subiaco where he made his home in a nearby cave. A neighboring monk is said to have supplied him with meager food and a rough cloak. At this time he could hardly have been more than twenty years of age, yet for the next three years he passed his days and nights in lonesome vigils and harsh self-discipline.

In the course of time the holy man was discovered by shepherds, who ministered to his simple needs and spread his fame over the countryside. He was temporarily lured away from his beloved cave by a request from a monastery in the vicinity to take the place of its recently deceased abbot. Benedict, suspecting that the monastery was lax in its discipline, hesitated to accept the invitation. Finally he yielded, but his severity so displeased the monks that they tried to poison him. Discovering their attempt, he left them to their own devices and returned to the shelter of his cave. But he was soon robbed of his privacy. His reputation had traveled even to Rome. People of distinction brought him their sons for training, while devotees attached themselves to his person, thus making necessary the establishment of a monastic community. Within a few years twelve groups, each composed of twelve members and presided over by an abbot whom Benedict appointed, had been set up, and all were under the close observation of the founder.

The jealousy of local priests, resulting in persecution, led Benedict to select a few companions and seek a new abode. He journeyed southward until he arrived at the ruins of Cassinum, once the site of a military colony, half way between Rome and Naples. The town lay at the foot of a hill crowned by a grove sacred to Apollo. The wanderers ascended the hill, used the trees for building purposes, destroyed the idol and altar of Apollo, and there set up a monastic establishment, the famous Monte Cassino, where Benedict was to remain the rest of his life. The time of its founding may be placed roughly in the period of 525-530 A.D., and Benedict's death is commonly supposed to have occurred not long after 542 A.D.

The story of the years spent at Monte Cassino has been so adorned with miracles and extravagant legends that a sober reconstruction of its details is no longer possible. But the main items are still recoverable. Benedict lived quite undisturbed by the political events of the times. Since the year 489 the Ostrogoths had been in possession of Italy. Under their king Theodoric (493-526) the government was more stable and efficient than it had been during the greater part of the previous century. Even the disturbances of the stormy years following Theodoric's death scarcely touched the monks in the seclusion of their mountain home. Armies swept back and forth upon the plains below, while Benedict toiled in the fields with his companions, sat reading at the gate of the monastery, recited prayers and sang psalms at the canonical hours, or superintended other phases of the community life in accordance with his elaborate *Rule* designed to discipline the soul in "divine servitude."

Benedict's importance for western Christendom lay in his genius for monastic organization. He was never involved in political struggles, doctrinal disputes, or problems of ecclesiastical administration such as had taxed the powers of Leo. Yet Benedict's talent for generalship was none the less apparent, nor was his gift to the church any less significant. Monasticism now was in sore need of an organizing genius who could set its house in order. This Benedict did. The full value of his work was not realized in his lifetime, and was perhaps hardly suspected even by himself, but in later years it became abundantly evident.

The Christian world was full of monks in the sixth century. The practice of withdrawing from normal social contacts in order to cultivate in solitude a higher degree of personal piety had sprung up in Egypt during the third century. Antony was the revered exemplar of this anchoretic ideal. In the early fourth century another Egyptian, Pachomius, had gathered monks into communities, organized as agricultural and industrial colonies with a well-defined form of government. There are said to have been ten of these houses, nine for men and one for women, with about 7,000 inmates, in the Egyptian monasteries when Pachomius died in 346 A.D. In Palestine, Syria and Asia the individual ascetic, like Simeon Stylites in the fifth century, was greatly admired. There were also monastic communities, such as we have already met in Cappadocia under the direction of Eustathius of Sebaste and Basil of Cæsarea and in Bethlehem under Jerome and Paula. Gaul also had been a fertile soil for the growth of the movement, with Martin at Tours, John Cassian at Marseilles, and Cæsarius at Arles as outstanding leaders.

Various motives induced Christians to become monks and nuns. There was a widespread distrust of society in those times; pious souls grew world-weary and longed to anticipate their release. There were good reasons for this state of feeling. The church persistently urged its members to fix their gaze on the future and prepare their souls for the life beyond the grave. Escape from earth and its afflictions, from the life of the sinful flesh and its desires, and ascent to the perfect bliss of heaven in the presence of the holy God, was the faithful Christian's supreme ambition. The world surrounded him with evils that tarnished his soul. Roman life was honeycombed by heathen customs that plagued the church even for long years after it had become the legal religion of the state. As the official cult of the Empire, Christianity was forced into worldliness and the moral quality of its community life fell to lower levels. It was no longer a congregation of saints, but an assembly of sinners presumed to be on the way to sainthood but not always eager to hasten their progress. Restive spirits sought a more rigorous discipline in austere solitude or monastic fellowship.

Also, the ecclesiastical institution was "in the world," and more or less involved in its sinfulness and distresses. It suffered from the ravages wrought by war and the disruption of governments. It could not protect its members from loss of their property when the plundering barbarians swarmed over a country nor could it stay the deadly hand of famine and pestilence that followed in the wake of war. Home, friends and family estates might vanish overnight in spite of the protection offered by the church. Was it not the sensible thing for Christians to withdraw as much as possible from ordinary social contacts? At the time of Alaric's invasion Jerome quite naturally wrote to one of his lady friends, "Dearest daughter in Christ, will you marry amid such scenes as these?" By fleeing from contemporary society the monk started eagerly on his journey to heaven. He almost took it by violence, forcing his way into the kingdom well in advance of his deliverance from the world by death.

In reality monasticism, by the time of Benedict, had come to constitute a distinctive phase of the Christian enterprise side by side with its ecclesiastical institutions. Yet monks were still largely a law unto themselves, whether they lived in solitude or in groups. Their discipline might be extremely severe or grossly lax. They had fled one world only to find themselves in another of their own making where they were subject to new temptations that ever lay in wait for the unwary. Some of them, growing inordinately proud of their holiness, exploited sanctity for their own profit. Moral irregularities occasionally crept into their simple society. Monasticism had behind it a mighty moral force but its energy needed to be brought under better control and to be more consistently directed toward functional ends. The situation called for the services of a capable organizer. While Benedict worked out regulations for his own monastery only, the depth of his insight, the sanity of his judgments, and the breadth of his vision, as embodied in his *Rule*, became a common possession of western monasticism and raised it to a position of renewed power and usefulness.

Looking upon the youthful Benedict living alone in his cave, one would not easily have seen in him the master mind of a great organizer. · As the years passed he had been making some valuable observations. He was led to distinguish sharply between different sorts of monks, on whom he pronounced keen judgments. One type, the "vagrants" as he called them, traveled about from place to place "serving their own pleasures and the allurements of the palate." These he heartily denounced. Another class, the "sarabites," lived in companies of two or three without an overseer and under no discipline. These also were disapproved. The "anchoret" who dwelt alone in some remote place was less culpable but should not be encouraged. The ideal monk was the "cenobite" who shared in the common life of a group presided over by a head, the abbot ("father"), and subject to specific regulations. This was the truly commendable form of monasticism, for which Benedict prepared his *Rule*.

Benedict made the entire life of the monastic society conform to three fundamental principles. These were absolute obedience, simplicity in living, and constant occupation. Rigid though the demands were, they were seasoned by moderation. Rules were not to be kept for their own sake, hence reasonable exceptions were necessary for practical ends. Excessive austerities were eliminated, special conditions were recognized, and high ideals of attainment were kept continually in the foreground of attention. No summary of the *Rule* can be substituted for a reading of the document in its entirety, but a few sentences relating to the authority of the superior over the monks will serve to illustrate its temper: "As often as any matters of special importance have to be transacted in the monastery let the abbot call together the whole congregation and himself state the problem in hand. After he has heard the advice of the brethren, let him ponder it by himself, and do what he considers most expedient. We have said that all ought to be called to take counsel, because the Lord often reveals to a younger member what is best. So let the brethren give advice with all humble subjection and presume not impudently to defend what seems good to them, but rather let the matter be left to the judgment of the abbot, so that they may all be obedient to what he deems best. But just as it becomes the disciples to obey the master, so also it is seemly for him to dispose of all things prudently and justly" (Chap. III).

Obedience to the *Rule* was not the end, but only the

beginning of the religious way. Those who would attain to perfection must study the Scriptures, since these writings furnish the most complete rule of human life. One ought also to read the "holy fathers," especially Basil, to find examples of virtue and obedience. Therefore, "whosoever thou art who hastens toward the heavenly country, do thou first by the help of Christ carry out in full this *Rule* that we have written for beginners, and then at length thou shalt come, God guiding thee, to the lofty heights of learning and virtue which we have previously mentioned."

As the founder of the great Benedictine order whose influence was to spread widely over Europe, ultimately bringing other foundations under the control of its wise and beneficent rule, Benedict of Nursia deserves a place beside Leo the Great as a statesman of western Christendom. He brought order into the incoherent mass of ascetic ideals and practices then current and, working from within rather than from above, introduced into the monastic movement a sense of direction and a respect for organization that gave it fresh strength to endure and new power to serve the needs of the Christian world in the realms of industry, learning, and simple piety.

Gregory the Great

Gregory, born of patrician parents in Rome about the year 540, lived in a calamitous age. During the last three quarters of the sixth century political and social chaos reigned in Italy. The orderly government of Theodoric came to an end with his death in 526 A.D.. For the next ten years the Goths fought among themselves over the succession, until the army of the eastern emperor, Justinian, landed to undertake the reconquest of Italy. Then fol-

lowed almost two decades of continuous strife that deluged
the country in blood and devastated it with fire, famine and
pestilence, before the Goths were finally crushed in 553 A.D.
Five million people are said to have perished during this
period, and the principal cities, like Naples, Rome and
Milan, were left sadly despoiled and almost completely
depopulated. Between the years 546 and 552 Rome had
stood siege by one or another of the belligerents on five
different occasions. Gregory carried through life the memory of these terrible experiences from the days of his boyhood.

Although Italy continued to be ruled from Constantinople for the next decade and a half, the country remained
in a sorry condition. The imperial agents were harsh and
vexatious. They laid heavy taxes on the impoverished population, while they instituted only feeble measures to stimulate agriculture or to remedy the general economic distress.
Justinian was more interested in restoring the depleted
aristocracy of Italy and in adorning Catholic churches than
in reëstablishing society on a sound self-sustaining economic
basis. The farmers lacked instruments for cultivating the
soil, industry and commerce in the towns underwent no
revival, taxation was deadly, the middle class still further
declined, and the people appealed in vain to the emperor to
relieve them from the "impossibility of paying their debts."
While his officials and favorites battened on their pitiless
exactions, the rank and file of the scant population sank
only the more deeply into despair.

In the year 568 a new calamity befell Italy. The barbarian Lombards, breaking through from the north, began
their conquest of the country, to which the imperial authorities were unable to offer any serious resistance. The in-

vaders had as yet no strong political organization and were content to settle in the more easily accessible country districts, while the larger fortified towns and their contiguous territories remained for the most part under imperial control. Ravenna, Genoa, Rome, Naples and the regions immediately surrounding these cities continued in possession of the eastern emperor, while the various Lombard dukes set up their own little independent kingdoms in other parts of the country. But as their power increased and a central government developed, their presence in Italy became more uncomfortable for the native inhabitants, who vainly petitioned the rulers at Constantinople to suppress the intruders. Their depredations in Italy furnished Gregory some of his most troublesome problems.

In these unhappy times the Roman church, rather than the imperial palace at Constantinople, gave to Italy the leader whose statesmanship was equal to the occasion. By education and experience Gregory had been especially fitted in his youth and early manhood for the work he was later to perform. The family seems to have had a devout attachment to Catholic Christianity, an attitude not uncommon in those days among the nobility at Rome. Two of his father's sisters were nuns, and his mother also took the veil when she became a widow. Gregory was given the best education available, according to the standards then prevailing at Rome. Grammar and rhetoric were the fundamental disciplines, in which the boy received the customary training, although he never acquired the taste for ornamental discourse that had allured Christian scholars in the previous century. In fact, he spoke somewhat disdainfully of the rhetorician's skill and boasted of his own simplicity in style. One of his biographers praised him as a

master in the philosopher's art, but it was his acquaintance
with divine wisdom rather than his competency in dialectic
that gave him this distinction.

Gregory is said to have been "from his very youth devoted to God," yet evidently he was educated for a secular
career, probably for the legal profession, that especially attracted young men of the wealthy nobility in Rome.   In
this he seems to have been eminently successful.   He first
appears in the clear light of history as prefect of Rome, the
most important administrative office in the city, when he is
still in his early thirties.   About this time, his father having
died, Gregory inherited much property.   With a new sense
of responsibility he began to reflect more seriously upon
the question of a worthy mission in life.   Should he pursue
the futilities of worldly ambition by wasting time and
strength on temporal affairs in a decadent society that
seemed foredoomed to ultimate destruction?   Augustine's
vision of a thousand years of prosperity for the City of
God, gradually absorbing or supplanting the functions of
the earthly city, was no longer tenable.   Gregory was confident that the disasters of the times presaged an early end
of the present world.   Italy was desolate and even the
once glorious Rome was hardly more than a heap of ruins.
Under these circumstances one's supreme ambition should
be to prepare the soul for heaven.

Suddenly Gregory decided to change his course—experienced, as he calls it, his "conversion."   He retired from
public life and transformed the ancestral mansion at Rome
into a monastery (St. Andrew) where for three years he
lived in seclusion, subjecting himself to austerities that permanently impaired his health, studying the Scriptures and

other religious books, and ministering to the needs of his suffering fellow-citizens.

Since in later years he expressed enthusiastic admiration for the *Rule* of Benedict, we may assume that it had from the start been largely determinative for life in Gregory's monastic establishment at Rome. He was, however, so zealous in his quest for perfection that little regard was paid to moderation. Abstinence from food and sleep, supported by fervent prayer, seems to have been regarded as especially meritorious. Gregory narrates one of his experiences illustrating the miraculous effect produced by this state of mind. Once, as Easter approached, he was so ill that death seemed inevitable if he should refrain from taking any nourishment on the "sacred Sabbath" when all pious people ordinarily kept a complete fast. The prospect of having to violate the sacred custom filled him with great sorrow. He sought relief in prayer: "It suddenly occurred to me to take Eleutherius, the man of God, privately with me to the oratory and beg of him to obtain by his prayers from Almighty God that I might receive power to fast on that day. This I did. As soon as we entered the oratory he began at my humble request to pray earnestly with tears. After a short time his prayer ended and he left the oratory. But when he pronounced the benediction over me my stomach at once received such strength that all thought of food and feeling of sickness utterly vanished."

Gregory was not allowed to remain permanently within the shelter of his monastery. The church needed men of his legal training, administrative ability and political experience to guide its destinies in one of the most trying periods of its history. The Lombards, growing more powerful, were spreading terror among the Italian people, plundering private and ecclesiastical properties, and even threatening to sack Rome. In vain the city sent messengers to Constantinople requesting troops for the protection of life and property. As usual, famine and pestilence attended the political disorders. Amid these scenes of distress Gregory was summoned by the pope to accept ordination as one of the seven deacons responsible for the administration of the seven regions into which Rome had been divided. Gregory assumed his new duties late in the year 578, or early in the following year. Temporarily he was compelled to leave the blessed and much coveted seclusion of his beloved St. Andrew's. While the remainder of his life was spent in public service for the church, he never lost sight of his monastic ideals. The supreme task of the church, like that of the monastery, was to prepare souls for another world.

Pelagius II became pope at Rome in the year 579. The city was feebly garrisoned, the aggressions of the Lombards had increased, and an embassy sent to Constantinople to solicit assistance had accomplished nothing. The pope determined to make a more urgent appeal to the emperor. Gregory was appointed the permanent papal ambassador at the imperial court, his chief responsibility being to secure military aid for the church in Italy. In this attempt he utterly failed, although he remained six years at the eastern capital, but in the meantime he accomplished other results that were of no slight significance for the future of the Roman church. He gained an insight into the weakness of imperial government that impressed upon him the necessity for the western church to undertake on its own account an aggressive political policy in Italy. He made the acquaintance of other resident or visiting ecclesiastics of note, like John "The Faster," Anastasius of Antioch, and Leander of Seville. He also had leisure to pursue Scriptural studies and participate in theological controversies that added to his prestige when later he became pope. But all the while he suffered under the serious handicap of complete ignorance of the Greek language, a defect which he seems to have made no attempt to remove. In this attitude there is, perhaps, an indication of the extent to which the Christianity of the West had already come to feel its essential separation from the churches of the East.

After returning to Rome Gregory enjoyed a few years of comparative peace in his monastery where he labored diligently at Biblical studies, bringing to completion his notable expositions of the Book of Job, the *Moralia,* that had been begun in Constantinople at the request of his fellow-monks and of his friend Leander of Seville. The modern reader may sometimes grow weary of Gregory's prolixity, for he purposely allowed his comments "to flow like a river" in order to edify his audience, a feature that was entirely congenial to the contemplative monk of the sixth century. The attractiveness of the work lay in its practical moral emphasis and the comfort it brought to yearning souls struggling "to drive away from the depths of one's heart the torment of earthly desires, to fix one's gaze upon the soul's eternal fatherland, and to breathe only the love of spiritual tranquillity." It was well designed to become the popular classic that it was in the Middle Ages.

Gregory was now the abbot of St. Andrew's, where he had established a veritable "school of saints" that gave to the church a future bishop of Syracuse, an archbishop of Ravenna, a bishop of Gallipoli, and Augustine, who led the band of missionaries sent to evangelize the Anglo-Saxons in Britain. Gregory also rendered much assistance to Pelagius II whom he appears to have served as papal secretary and at whose request he wrote a masterful treatise on the orthodox creed for the correction and guidance of the bishops of Istria. Gregory had no liking for theological dialectics but he had the characteristically Roman respect for authority and insisted, as Leo had done, that individual differences of opinion should be suppressed in the interests of ecclesiastical unity. What the basis of that unity should be, the successor of Peter alone could declare.

Rome was visited by a frightful plague in the year 590. It carried off Pope Pelagius II and the people chose Gregory to succeed him. In due time the election was confirmed by the eastern emperor and Gregory, much against his inclinations, was forced once more to abandon his monastic sanctuary. The prospect was not inviting. The plague had left the Roman population much depleted; a recent invasion of Italy by the Franks, although it had been successfully resisted by the Lombards, had rendered large sections of the country more desolate than ever; and the victors had grown doubly arrogant in their ambition to conquer all of Italy. Gregory undertook his new duties "with a sick heart." It was no empty rhetoric masquerading under the cloak of humility that prompted him to write to the emperor's sister: "I have lost the deep joy of my quiet, and while I seem outwardly to have risen, I am inwardly debased. Wherefore I grieve that I am driven from the face of my Creator." The world seemed nearing its end, and the church was like an old ship whose rotten planks and creaking timbers could not withstand much longer the violence of the storms that were beating upon it from all quarters. With real regret Gregory left his monastery to occupy the papal chair at Rome and thereby to prove himself the greatest ecclesiastical statesman that Christendom had yet known.

When Gregory took the helm the church, as a physical phenomenon, might seem to resemble a weather-beaten derelict almost ready to sink, but while the present order of the world endured the supreme mission of the church was to bear the souls of men to their eternal haven. God had established Christianity for this specific purpose, and a bishop who occupied the Roman see continued to discharge the responsibility that Christ had delegated to Peter. The pope had a two-fold task. He must lead the church, particularly the Roman church, forward to the mastery of its environment on all fronts; and, strengthening it from within, he must make it a complete and perfect institution sufficient for the needs of mankind in the midst of a crumbling political and social order.

Gregory was still under the sway of the imperial ideal inherited by Christendom from the Constantinian age. Since church and state were inseparable, it was the God-imposed duty of emperors to protect the church, enforce its approved doctrines, and defend its properties. Repeatedly Gregory appealed to the eastern ruler, Maurice, to come to the aid of Peter's successor. But when the emperor failed to meet his obligations, the pope was compelled himself to assume this secular duty. Practically ignoring the weaklings who represented the emperor at Ravenna, Gregory ruled at Rome as governor of both church and state. When forced by necessity, he used ecclesiastical money to bribe the Lombards, he entered into treaty relations with a Lombard duke or king regardless of the wishes of the exarch at Ravenna, and he appointed a military officer to command the garrison at Naples. He assumed it to be his function to protect life and property, since the princes had failed to obey his summons to perform their proper task. Nor did he restrict this activity to Italy. When the occasion required, he assumed the right to conduct political negotiations in any part of western Europe, just as he claimed an authority from God superior even to that of the eastern emperor.

Gregory's care for the orderly conduct, morality, and sound doctrine of the churches was exceedingly conscientious. He insisted on meticulous accuracy in all ecclesiastical bookkeeping, which was no small undertaking in those days when the church owned vast properties. Nor was he less exacting in the matter of elections, clerical duties, and ritual. Over neighboring bishops he ruled with a strong, though usually gentle, hand. He sought to secure universal obedience to the authority of Rome, not for the explicit purpose of making his power conspicuous, but in order to insure the efficiency of the church as a saving institution.

Masterful as was Gregory's administration, he was none the less eminent as a moral force in Christianity. To a degree almost uncanny, he combined in one person the distinguishing traits of both Leo and Benedict. The religiosity of the monk characterized him throughout his career as pope. In his many sermons his controlling purpose was to be understood by the common people to whose varying needs he sought to minister. His boundless faith in the miraculous and his fondness for apt illustration placed him on common ground with even his most illiterate parishioners. As a pastor his main stress was on the care of souls.

This, he insisted, was the first duty of every bishop, whatever the dignity of his see. Gregory's *Pastoral Rule*, in many respects the choicest of all his writings, attempts to do for bishops what Benedict's *Rule* aimed to do for monks, and it enjoyed a similarly wide popularity in the later church. As a handbook for pastors, it is still deserving of serious consideration. Gregory would have the shepherd of souls equipped in knowledge and strong in character, a living example of the piety he demands in the members of his flock. He must be competent to teach others but he should also be aware of his own infirmities and of his constant need of divine help in the discharge of his multitudinous duties.

Though broken in health, and often unable to rise from his couch for weeks in succession, Gregory's mind was incessantly active. He labored indefatigably until his frail body finally succumbed to death in the year 604. An ancient biographer says of him that he never rested, but was "ever engaged in providing for the interests of his people, or in composing some writing worthy of the church, or in searching out the secrets of heaven by the grace of contemplation." To secular affairs in Rome he was as diligently attentive while pope as he had previously been when prefect. The charities of the church were his constant care. Preaching to the common people was an activity always dear to him. The minutest details of parish work in all the churches were always given careful consideration. And he never relaxed his vigilance over the temporal and spiritual welfare of Christendom so far as it came within the reach of his voice and his pen.

The administrative vision of Leo and the moral earnestness of Benedict were perpetuated and became a more substantial heritage of the western church through the work of Gregory. He made more concretely real the supremacy of the Roman see as an establishment of Christ founded on Peter, and the only gate to heaven—the church to which all bishops and princes were bound to submit. If Leo is to be called the founder of the medieval papacy, Gregory may be termed the creator of medieval Catholicism.

CHAPTER VIII

LEADERS ON NEW FRONTIERS

While Christian leaders were striving to maintain the prestige of the church in Italy, its status in the countries beyond the Alps was even more precarious.

In Spain, where the Visigoths set up their kingdom, Catholic Christianity was already firmly established and continued to exist side by side with the Arian church of the barbarian invaders. They were always a minority, as compared with the native Spanish-Roman population, and their princes generally refrained from vigorous attacks upon the Catholic elements in society. Repressive measures were sometimes employed in the earlier period of the Visigothic occupation, but before the sixth century had ended King Reccared espoused the Catholic faith and legalized it in his domains. Leander, the archbishop of Seville, and especially his successor, the learned Isidore, who held office from 600 to 636, conducted the affairs of the church without serious interference from the state. At the same time, however, ecclesiastical activities were subject to the will of the king, who summoned councils, appointed or deposed bishops, and made the church virtually a national institution, until the conquest of the Moslems in 711 A.D. ended Visigothic rule and temporarily halted the growth of Spanish Christianity.

In Roman times Christianity had been sparsely planted in the British Isles. Since the middle of the third century there had been churches in Britain, whence the religion had spread to Wales, Ireland, and Scotland, where it was taken up by the native Celtic population during the fifth century. Early in this period, Patrick, who had been a monk in the famous establishment at Lerins, an island south of Gaul, did missionary work in Ireland. About the year 565 Columba, who has been called the "apostle to Caledonia," founded his noted monastery at Iona, from which Christianity was carried to Scotland and northern England. But these Christian beginnings were seriously arrested by the coming of the heathen Anglo-Saxons who had settled in Britain soon after the middle of the fifth century. Primitive British Christianity, to which the conquerors remained hostile, survived in comparative isolation in the western and northern sections of the islands, while the conversion of the Anglo-Saxons awaited the coming of Augustine and his companions from Rome in the time of Gregory the Great.

Gaul was the arena in which the new developments of the Christian movement in western Europe were to be the most vividly and significantly displayed. The leaders of the church were confronted by a perplexing array of diverse problems. They found themselves involved in the rivalries of various groups among the new settlers contending with one another for possession of the country. With the exception of the Franks, the barbarian invaders were at first Arians, and made this church the official religion in their kingdoms, greatly to the distress of the original Gallo-Roman Catholic Christians. The old Gallic heathenism, infused with large elements of Roman paganism, also lingered on beside Christianity and was supplemented by new accretions derived from Franks and Teutons. Furthermore, Christendom in Gaul had not yet acquired the organic solidarity that might have made possible greater unity and concentration of effort. There were powerful churches with able bishops at important points, but Gaul had no Petrine see, no dominating ecclesiastical center, and the authority of the Roman church was not yet established west of the Alps.

Both politically and religiously, sectionalism characterized society in Gaul, and ecclesiastics expended a large part of their time and energy negotiating with rival nobles or princes in order to protect the property of the parish, and minister to local needs. Under these conditions leaders often represented the aristocratic type of cleric, a high-born and wealthy person, who had remarkable political and administrative ability, and who rendered indispensable service to the church in the larger cities, as did Sidonius Apollinaris in Auvergne, or Gregory at Tours. Christian monasticism had also spread widely over Gaul even before the barbarian invasions, and it continued to flourish in the succeeding years. But, being highly individualistic and diversified in its forms, it could make no substantial contribution toward the unification of Gallic Christendom until it discovered a new Benedict, whom it ultimately found in the person of Boniface. On the new political frontier the church in Gaul early made important converts, notably Clovis, king of the Franks, who, along with some three thousand of his soldiers, was baptized at Rheims on Christmas Day in the year 496. But a barbarian ruler capable of restoring to the church of the West the imperial protection that it had lost with the fall of the western Roman Empire was not realized until the time of Charlemagne.

GREGORY OF TOURS

Gregory represents a class of Christian leaders who guided the destinies of the church during the perilous years of transition from Roman to Frankish domination in Gaul. These men were rooted more or less firmly in the passing Roman culture, while their constructive labors were conditioned mainly by the newly arising barbarian society. Gregory, born probably in the year 538, belonged to a prosperous senatorial family residing at Clermont (Auvergne). In the case of his fellow-countryman Sidonius Apollinaris, who had been bishop of Clermont in the previous century (471-489), Roman heritages were chiefly influential in the making of the cleric, but by Gregory's day the balances had tipped strongly in the direction of Gallicanism.

Gregory's parents were loyal Catholics, and many of his relatives had been bishops. When he held the see of Tours he could note with some pride that he was related by blood to all but five of its previous eighteen occupants over a period of two centuries. His baptismal name had been Georgius Florentius, but later he piously took the name of Gregory, out of respect for his famous great-grandfather, the bishop of Langres. His grand-uncle, Nicetius, was bishop of Lyons, his uncle was bishop of Clermont, and he was preceded at Tours by his cousin Eufronius. It might seem that Gregory had been destined from birth for the episcopacy, but this prospect does not seem to have been determinative for his early life. As was the custom of the times, he received his education in the church, where he imbibed some secular and Scriptural learning, along with a prodigious faith in the miraculous efficacy of the saints.

As a boy Gregory exemplified a simple piety, marked by the credulity characteristic of the age. On one occasion he cured his father of gout by placing under the sick man's pillow a chip of wood on which the name "Joshua," revealed to Gregory in a dream, had been inscribed. The boy himself suffered from poor health. Once when seized by a severe attack of gastric fever his end seemed near. But, inspired by a "divine suggestion," he asked that he be taken to the tomb of a certain saint. On recovering from the illness he kept a vow he had made at the time to devote himself to the religious life. Frequent recurrences of fever seem never to have aroused in his mind any suspicions as to the therapeutic powers of the saints. In early manhood when death again threatened him he was carried to the tomb of Martin at Tours where he kept a vigil that restored his appetite and revived his strength. But his rebellious stomach was a perpetual trouble-maker, which the local doctors were unable to master. Gregory, disdainful of their feeble efforts, resorted at such times to his favorite tonic, a potion made of dust from the shrine of the saint; or he rubbed his abdomen with a cloth hung at the tomb.

Throughout his career he retained his simple faith in the limitless power of deceased saints and the prophylactic energy of objects that had come in contact with their graves. He always wore suspended from a string about his neck a bag of relics whose mere elevation would quell a tempest. Brigands could be resisted and plunged into headlong flight by the invocation of the saintly Martin. A quantity of dust from this saint's tomb was always in Gregory's medicine kit ready for use in curing fever or dysentery, maladies that frequently overtook the bishop and his attendants when on a journey under the unsanitary conditions of those times.

One marvels that a man who, according to modern standards, was so enslaved to superstition, could have displayed Gregory's sturdy morality, strength of character, firmness of purpose, indomitable courage, and statesmanlike skill in dealing with contemporaries who held high positions and authority in both church and state.

In the year 573 Gregory became bishop of Tours, having been chosen by the clergy and the people, and approved by the Frankish king Sigebert to whose territory the city at that time belonged. The office involved its holder in many difficulties, not the least of which was the political problem. When Clovis had died in 511 A.D. the united kingdom of the Franks was divided among his descendants. In Gregory's day there were three principal divisions of territory, each held by a prince jealous of the others and ever ready to invade a rival's domains. The northeastern area (Austrasia) was ruled by Sigebert and his famous wife Brunhild. Neustria, to the northwest, was governed by Chilperic, who was largely dominated by a vicious and scheming concubine, Fredegund. Burgundy, in the south, was subject to the weak and vacillating Guntram. Tours was so situated that it was a constant bone of contention among these warring princes, and Gregory suffered severely from their machinations.

During the first two years of Gregory's episcopacy, while Tours remained under the control of Sigebert, the bishop enjoyed comparative peace in the administration of his ecclesiastical duties. Then Sigebert fell a victim to assassins inspired by the wicked Fredegund and Tours was annexed to the kingdom of Chilperic. This event marked the beginning of a long series of difficulties for Gregory during which his moral and administrative abilities were subjected to the severest tests. Chilperic was, unquestionably, the "worst king in Gaul," and his queen was one of the most unprincipled of women, even in an age when expediency was all too readily regarded as an essential virtue.

Chilperic was superstitious, but thought himself so skilful in the use of relics and in the reading of portents that he could outwit God without the aid of a Christian bishop. The king neither feared nor respected the church, which was therefore unable to place any restraint upon the royal passions and perversities. Oppressive taxes were imposed upon his subjects as a means of satisfying Chilperic's greed. He would elevate to the episcopacy the candidate who could furnish the largest bribe, even though he were an untrained layman. Property willed to the churches was diverted to the king, who looked with covetous eyes upon the wealth of the ecclesiastical institution. His avarice phrased itself in the lament: "Our treasury is empty, all our riches have passed over to the churches; the bishops alone reign; our power is gone; it has been transferred to the bishops of the cities." In dealing with this type of ruler, Gregory found himself involved in numerous tasks far less congenial than those of his ministrations to the flock that he ordinarily shepherded. The distinction of Tours as a religious center in Gaul was eminent and its bishop's responsibilities were correspondingly great. His duty was to preserve the integrity of church properties, to resist the appointments of unworthy men to clerical offices, to protest against the debauchery and chicanery practiced at the court, and to shield as best he could both clergy and laity from the injustice and cruelty of the autocratic political rulers.

Both Chilperic and Fredegund found Gregory an inconvenient person with whom to deal. Therefore they planned to rid themselves of him. The conflict came about over Gregory's efforts on behalf of the bishop of Rouen, Prætextatus, who had incurred the displeasure of the queen. Gregory was summoned into the king's presence and accused of consenting to iniquity by defending a fellow-bishop whom the royal authority condemned. It was clearly intimated that his allegiance to the king required a different course of action, else the bishop would be held guilty of lese majesty. To this Gregory replied: "O king, if any of the rest of us strays from the path of justice, thou art there to correct him. But if thou goest astray, who shall censure thee?" Thus Gregory stood firmly upon his rights as the spokesman of Heaven and threatened the king with the judgment of God. When Fredegund tried her wiles upon the bishop she met a similar rebuff. She offered him two hundred pounds of silver if he would yield to her wishes, as, so she affirmed, every other bishop had promised to do. To this temptation Gregory curtly replied: "If you gave me a thousand pounds of gold and silver, what could I do but obey the command of the Lord?"

Gregory's enemies were not always persons of the royal court; some of his sorest trials were occasioned by treachery within his own ecclesiastical household. An ambitious local priest, Riculfus, and a sub-deacon of the same name joined forces with an unscrupulous local count to discredit Gregory in the eyes of Chilperic and secure his removal from office. The unfaithful priest was to take over the bishop's office while the sub-deacon was to be elevated to the dignity of archdeacon. The plotters reported that Gregory had slandered the queen by saying that she was the mistress of Bertram the archbishop of Bordeaux. Enemies diligently fed the flames of suspicion until Gregory was forced to declare his innocence before a council of bishops held at the royal villa of Berny in the summer of 580. Bertram, an aristocratic and wealthy prelate, who was also a favorite at the court of Chilperic, presided over the council and made the proceedings as embarrassing as possible for the accused bishop. But popular feeling was on his side and, although he was subjected to the indignity of having to declare three times by solemn oath that he had never spoken against the honor of the queen, he was finally acquitted.

During Gregory's absence the self-confident Riculfus had installed himself in the episcopal office, had taken possession of the property of the church, and had generously distributed largess in the form of fields or vineyards among the higher clergy. He was prepared to resist the rightful bishop when he returned. But the latter, loved and revered by the people, soon reëstablished his authority and incarcerated Riculfus in a monastery, from which he was presently rescued through deceptive methods employed by Felix, bishop of Nantes, another prelate of aristocratic birth and a bitter enemy of Gregory.

Such events are typical of the many conflicts experienced by Gregory in both church and state. The strain was somewhat relieved when, after Chilperic's assassination in the year 585, Tours came into the possession of Guntram, king of Burgundy. Two years later it became again a part of Austrasia, now ruled by Sigebert's young son, Childebert II, but actually controlled by the queen-mother, Brunhild. Gregory's authority was no longer disputed, but he was never free from worries occasioned by the political disturbances of the age and the lack of harmony among the contemporary bishops. Tax-collectors constantly menaced the estates of the church; questionable practices among the clergy caused ceaseless anxiety; earthquakes, famines and pestilence were perpetual enemies; "false Christs" were ever ready to prey upon the gullibility of the ignorant populace; and dangerous journeys had to be undertaken in the interests of the church and its holdings in different parts of the country where the conditions of travel were both difficult and hazardous.

Gregory's cares were always abundant. Yet he accomplished many constructive labors. He was ever restoring and beautifying churches. He industriously unearthed hidden relics, making them available for the healing of afflicted people. Monasteries also received his diligent attention, while the physical and moral well-being of his flock was always dear to his heart. Amid all of these activities he found time to compose numerous books, not in order to produce fine literature—he apologetically disclaimed any ability in this field of culture—but for practical purposes. His chief aim was to provide edification for the simple-minded people of his day. He compiled a book from the "Masses" of Sidonius, wrote a commentary on the psalms, made extensive contributions to hagiographical legends, and produced a *History of the Franks*, which, notwithstanding its diffuse style and monstrous credulities, remains for the modern historian his principal source of information on the period.

Even though Gregory may not be a towering figure among the great names in ecclesiastical history, he certainly was in his day a commanding personage among the leaders of the church on its new western frontiers. At the principal seat of religion in Gaul he piloted Christianity through heavy seas during one of the most stormy periods of its career. When he died, late in the year 594, he left to the

Frankish church the fragrant memory of his genuine piety, sturdy moral integrity, and devotion to his beloved institution.

BONIFACE

Boniface was a true child of the Roman Catholic Church of Britain that had arisen on the foundations laid by Augustine and his companions, whom Gregory the Great had commissioned to evangelize the Anglo-Saxons in the year 596. The date and place of Boniface's birth are not positively known, but the most probable opinion locates the event at the little village of Crediton in Devonshire about the year 680. Originally his name was Winfrid, and he was so called until the year 719, when the pope renamed him Boniface.

England was already a land of monasteries when Boniface was born. His parents belonged to the nobility of Wessex, where churches seem to have been as yet few in number but where the country was frequently visited by traveling missionaries who were entertained by the Christian parents of Boniface. The visitors captured the imagination of the boy, who at the age of seven prevailed upon his reluctant father to allow his son to enter the nearby monastery at Exeter. There the youth received his early education, and later pursued his studies at the abbey of Nutshall (or Nursling) near Winchester. He early became so distinguished for his learning that he was placed in charge of the abbey school. He proved to be a successful teacher as well as a devoted monk, and was elevated to the dignity of the priesthood when he reached the necessary age of thirty.

A brilliant future was now in prospect for Boniface in England, when suddenly he decided to become a missionary to the unconverted peoples of Germany. At the time his fellow-countryman, Willibrord, was preaching in Frisia (modern Holland) where, with the help of Frankish political influence, he had established headquarters at Utrecht. In the year 716 Boniface set out upon his new undertaking, but on arriving at Frisia he discovered that recent political changes had resulted in a hostile attitude toward the Franks and also toward the missionaries who were under Frankish protection. Willibrord had felt it necessary to leave Utrecht, and Boniface, after a short stay in the country, decided to return to England.

The missionary enterprise was not, however, abandoned. Although Boniface might now have become abbot of the monastery of Nutshall, he declined the honor, fortified himself with letters of recommendation from the diocesan bishop, Daniel of Winchester, and proceeded to Rome to consult the Pope, Gregory II, who was already interested in planting the church among the Germans. Boniface was given a hearty welcome in Rome, where he remained some months maturing his plans and receiving instructions from the papacy. In May, 719, the missionary set out for Germany bearing Gregory's blessing and his explicit injunction to teach the Germans to observe the Roman liturgical practices and to refer their difficult problems to the see of Peter for decision.

Boniface journeyed northward by easy stages through Bavaria and Thuringia toward Frisia. A change in political conditions had now made possible the return of Willibrord to Utrecht, with whom Boniface continued to labor for four years. He might have become the aged bishop's successor at Utrecht had he not felt an irrepressible urge to seek new frontiers. While Frankish rule had extended itself far beyond the right bank of the Rhine, the peoples living in these regions were still largely pagan and Boniface had set his heart on their conversion. Charles Martel was now in control of the kingdom of the Franks, and while he was not himself a zealous churchman, he was convinced that it was desirable to have his subjects embrace the Christian religion and live in accordance with the requirements of the church. He was ready, therefore, to support the evangelizing activities of Boniface. This help the missionary duly recognized several years later in a letter to Daniel of Winchester: "Without the patronage of the Prince of the Franks, I am able neither to rule the people of the church nor to defend the priests or deacons, the monks or nuns. And I am not sufficiently powerful to hinder the very rites of the pagans and the sacrileges of idols in Germany without his order and the dread of him." The relation of the missionary to the state authorities is not a peculiarly modern phase of the mission enterprise.

By means of messengers and correspondence, Boniface kept in close touch with the home base, both in England and in Rome. A letter from Daniel of Winchester, evidently written in answer to a request of Boniface, gives an idea of the missionary message of those days. Its main purpose was to turn the pagans from worship of their ancestral gods to acceptance of the Christian deity. Daniel counseled moderation and tact. He wrote: "It is not necessary to combat the heresy of the pagans directly, nor to contest the genealogy of their gods. One should rather proceed by discreet questions and let them explain their beliefs. Thus one will lead them to recognize that their gods have not always existed." The folly of pagan mythology should be refuted, not by denunciation, but by exhibiting the nobler quality of Christian doctrines. Thus the heathen "will be more ashamed than irritated by this indirect refutation of their false beliefs, and, furthermore, it is good to show them upon occasion that, even if one does combat their doctrines, one does not really ignore them." And the pagans' belief that their gods give them the greatest blessing was to be gently undermined. They were to be shown that Christians enjoyed divine favors in a much higher degree: "If the gods are all-powerful, benevolent, and just, they should recompense their worshipers and punish those who scorn them. But, then, how explain the prosperity of Christians, who have taken away almost the whole world and who are in possession of the richest and most fertile regions, leaving to the followers of the pagan gods only the frigid regions, where driven, one might say, from the entire earth, they keep only a semblance of rule? One should insist upon this point, that the Christians constitute almost the whole of humanity. In comparison with them, what is the little flock of idolaters who have remained faithful to the ancient heresy?"

The initial efforts of Boniface so satisfied the pope that he summoned him to Rome to receive episcopal ordination in the year 722. On the way back to his field, Boniface paid a visit to Charles Martel before returning to the scene of his former labors where he found the situation satisfactory. He could now proceed with even greater confidence. At this time occurred the picturesque incident of felling the sacred oak of Thor at Geismar. From now on the work of expansion and consolidation proceeded steadily. New regions in Thuringia were Christianized, churches and monasteries were established at various places, and such priests and converts as had formerly followed the less rigid Frankish Christian practices were forced to abandon their customs and adopt the rules that Boniface had received from the pope. A monastery recently founded at Ohrdruff became the episcopal residence of Boniface, whither fresh helpers came from England to assist the pioneer missionary in his growing work. Among the newcomers, who took their places at different stations and rendered invaluable service in the new fields, Lull is perhaps most worthy of mention.

In the year 731 Pope Gregory II died. His successor was Gregory III, to whom Boniface addressed a letter of felicitation. The pope responded by sending Boniface the *pallium*, which signified his elevation to the rank of archbishop. This honor was an intimation that he should add to his monastic and evangelizing labors the further duty of organizing parishes in the new territory with bishops stationed at the larger places, who would assemble at stated times to hold councils, and, under the supervision of the archbishop, organize the Christianity of Germany into a genuinely hierarchical institution subject to the Roman see. Boniface undertook the discharge of his new responsibilities first in Bavaria. This task occupied him for the next six years, when he made a third visit to Rome where he spent a whole year in close contact with the pope. When he left he was equipped with a precious treasure of relics to be distributed among the sanctuaries he had founded, and he carried with him a fresh supply of commendatory letters. He passed through Bavaria, where he confirmed and extended his previous work, and then moved on to Thuringia to initiate the hierarchical organization in that territory. Here the task was harder to accomplish than in Bavaria, where Roman influence was more readily accepted. But the archbishop labored assiduously and not without a fair measure of success. He founded several episcopal sees and introduced many reforms in harmony with the wishes of Rome.

In the year 741 Charles Martel died, as did also Pope Gregory III. The new pope, Zacharias, was as ready as his predecessors had been to accept the services of Boniface, who in his letter of felicitation to the pontiff wrote: "I will be to you a faithful and devoted servitor, and I shall not cease to bend all those whom God gives me as disciples, in the provinces which you have confided to me, to obedience to the Roman Church." Presently Boniface was able to make good this promise, not only on his proper mission field in Germany, but also within the Frankish church. For a long time he had felt grief and indignation over the irregularities among the clergy of the Franks under Charles Martel but he had been powerless to effect reforms that he would have liked to introduce in order to make Roman prestige more prevalent.

The kingdom of Charles passed to two of his sons, Carloman and Pepin. Both of them had been reared under strong monastic influence, and Carloman, after half a dozen years, surrendered his share in the government to found a monastery at Rome dedicated to Sylvester, the pope to whom tradition alleged that Constantine had made his famous "donation of Italy." Pepin was more inclined toward statesmanship but still bore the stamp of piety that had been placed upon him by his tutor-monks at St. Denis, and was readier than his father had been to befriend the pope in his struggles with the Lombards and to allow his legate, Boniface, a freer hand in the affairs of the Frankish church. Under Carloman in Austrasia and Pepin in Neustria Boniface's prestige was at its height. Since the year 743 his archiepiscopal residence had been Mainz, where he was within relatively easy reach of both Germany and France.

Boniface's efforts, backed by papal zeal, were directed toward the reconstitution of the hierarchical organization and the establishment of ecclesiastical unity by means of councils. In the years 742 and 743 Carloman convened synods in Austrasia, and a general council of the whole kingdom of the Franks was held in 745. In these gatherings, where Boniface's influence prevailed, important reforms were initiated. One line of action was aimed at restraining the worldliness of the Frankish clergy. They were forbidden to carry arms, to go to war, to hunt or to have falcons—restrictions that were quite out of line with their previous manner of life. Debauched ecclesiastics were to be deposed, imprisoned, and reduced to a diet of bread and water. The monasteries were brought under the *Rule* of Benedict. Pagan practices that had been absorbed into the church were to be eliminated. Reforms in the liturgy, to bring it more rigidly in line with Roman customs, were also attempted. Certain bishops charged with heresy were condemned. And, most difficult of all, an effort was made to recover for the church the properties that had been extensively confiscated in the time of Charles Martel.

In return for permission to push its ecclesiastical reforms, the church was able to render the prince of the Franks a very important service. With the retirement of his brother Pepin became the sole ruler, but in principle he was only a usurper. The descendants of Clovis, notwithstanding the loss of their power, were still the legitimate kings. Childeric III now held the title and Pepin sought some plausible means of setting the puppet aside. The Frankish nobles and populace were ready to acknowledge the kingship of Pepin, but the line of Clovis was presumed to have been of divine origin. The change proposed by Pepin needed, therefore, not only human approval but also the authentication of Heaven. This was secured by papal action. At an assembly of the Franks at Soisson in November, 751, episcopal consecration was conferred upon Pepin, Boniface, in all probability, performing the ceremony. In place of the old royal line of divine descent, the Franks now had both an elected and a divinely sanctioned monarch. Henceforth Pepin ruled "by the grace of God," even the Christian God.

Having completed these labors, Boniface returned to his first love. His heart had always been in his missionary work. All the while he had kept a watchful eye upon the prosperity of Christianity in Germany. In the year 751 he had obtained recognition for his new monastic foundation at Fulda, to which he was much devoted. Worn out by his many toils he desired to complete his ministry with a return to Frisia. In the year 753 he spent some time in the country, and the next year he set out again with a band of faithful companions to revisit those regions. Descending the Rhine the missionaries arrived one evening on the shores of the little river Borne. They had high hopes of receiving and confirming the newly baptized, but during the night they were set upon by assassins and slaughtered almost to a man. Thus Boniface won the martyr's crown on June 5, 754.

CHARLEMAGNE

Pepin's friendship for the church was perpetuated and made still more effective by his powerful son and successor Charles, now commonly known as Charlemagne (Charles the Great). As was usual among the Franks, on Pepin's death in 768 his kingdom was divided between his two sons, Carloman and Charles; but the death of the former in 771 left Charles without a rival and made possible an expansion of Frankish power that was to have mighty consequences for the history of Christianity in Europe.

In the year 754 Pepin had definitely assumed the rôle of protector of the church and its estates in Italy, where the aggressive Lombards had grown constantly more menacing to the pope and his ecclesiastical properties. Stephen III, who now held the Roman see, went in person to solicit the aid of the king of the Franks. Charles, then a boy only eleven years of age, had met the suppliant and conducted him to his father at Ponthion. The pontiff, pronouncing a blessing upon Pepin and his royal family, conferred upon him the honorary title of Roman "patrician." The king in return pledged himself to restore to the papacy "the rights and territories of the Roman Republic." Just what areas were specified in the agreement are today uncertain, but they constituted the famous "donation of Pepin." In the years that followed, the king made good his promise. Two invasions of Italy by Pepin resulted in adding extensively to the possessions of the pope and raised him to the dignity of a secular ruler.

The papacy was in no position to maintain its political power without the aid of the Franks. Nor was Charlemagne, when vigorously engaged in enlarging his domains, hesitant in undertaking the complete overthrow of the Lombards in Italy. His opportunity came in the year 773. He crossed the Alps, wiped out the kingdom of the Lombards, and forced their ruler to retire into a monastery. At this time Charlemagne paid his first visit to Rome where, impressed by the deference paid him by Pope Hadrian and the Roman clergy, he is said to have added to the control of the papacy all of the territories formerly belonging to of Lombards south of the River Po.

No sooner had his royal patron recrossed the Alps than the pope found himself again in difficulties. There was still a strong unconquered Lombard dukedom in southern Italy, the archbishop of Ravenna was ambitious to be independent of the pontiff in Rome, and the lower clergy were all too ready to display insubordination. When Hadrian died in 795, his successor, Leo III, was unequal to his new responsibilities. He almost lost his life in a disgraceful riot at Rome led by disgruntled members of his own clergy in the spring of 799, when he was left beaten and bleeding in the street. His assailants, it is said, had attempted to put out his eyes and cut out his tongue. Although he survived this maltreatment, he was unable to restore order and had to seek refuge with the duke of Spoleto. Later he made his way to France, where Charlemagne received him graciously and sent him back to Rome in November under royal protection. The next year, when Charlemagne came to Rome, there occurred one of the most memorable incidents in the history of western Christendom.

Charlemagne had grown up with the conviction that it was the duty of the king of the Franks to protect the bishop of Rome, whoever he might be, since the papacy had conferred the divine blessing upon Pepin. When the youthful Charlemagne had been crowned as a prospective successor to his father, he had promised the popes to be a friend to their friends and an enemy to their enemies. But he certainly interpreted this pledge in terms of service, rather than of obedience, to the papacy. He always regarded it proper for him to exercise supervision over the Roman bishops. Leo III when elected to office had readily conceded the overlordship of the king of the Franks, to whom Leo had pledged allegiance. This meant, in the psychology of a feudal age, that the pope was virtually the vassal of the king, whose duty it was to protect his clients. Charlemagne, having accepted the obligation, proceeded to Rome to examine and set in order the affairs of the church.

When Charlemagne had confirmed Leo's election he had strictly warned the new pope to conduct himself honorably and in accordance with the rules of the church. During Leo's troubles damaging reports about his character and conduct had been circulated by his enemies. Since the accusations needed to be carefully investigated, Charlemagne undertook the task in person. In solemn conclave Franks and Romans gathered at St. Peter's in Rome, where the pope took oath on the Gospels declaring himself innocent of the crimes that had been charged against him. A few days later, on December 25, 800, as the king arose from prayer in the church of St. Peter, Leo placed a crown upon his head and the entire assembly joined in the salute: "Life and victory to Charles, most pious Augustus, crowned by God, the great and peace-bringing Emperor." At last western Christendom had its own new Constantine.

The restoration of political stability was not the only gift of Charlemagne to the church. He was also a patron of learning. England had become the home of a new Christian culture nourished in the monastic and episcopal schools. In the seventh century Benedict Biscop, founder of the Wearmouth and Jarrow, had made five visits to Rome, returning each time with a fresh supply of books for the use of his monks. His most famous pupil was the Venerable Bede. In the same period the school of Canterbury rose to prominence under the efficient leadership of its African abbot Hadrian. At York Archbishop Egbert, who had been a pupil of Bede at Jarrow, developed a noted cathedral school that produced the distinguished Alcuin who was chosen by Charlemagne to lead the educational activities in the kingdom of the Franks.

Alcuin had become known to the Frankish rulers as early as the year 768, when he had gone thither on a mission for the archbishop of York. A decade later Charlemagne became more intimately acquainted with the English scholar, whom he met at Parma when Alcuin was returning from a visit to Rome. It was then that Charlemagne invited him to join the group of scholars whom the king was assembling at his court. Alcuin, complying with the request, became the leader in Charlemagne's palace school about the year 782. There he found himself associated with other learned men of the time—Peter of Pisa, Paul the Deacon, Paulinus the Grammarian—but Alcuin was easily superior to any of his associates.

Charlemagne was interested, not alone in the opportunity for personal acquaintance with these scholars; he desired also to effect the diffusion of learning throughout his kingdom, especially among the monasteries and the churches. Alcuin became, to use a modern phrase, the king's "minister of education" and head of the royal "university" at the court. In this school Charlemagne himself was a diligent pupil, in so far as he could find time for the pursuit of learning, but his chief aim was to provide education for those who were to render service to the church and the state. He is said to have lamented that "the study of letters had been well-nigh extinguished by the neglect of his ancestors," a calamity that he sought to remedy in the same energetic way in which he extended and consolidated his political power.

Alcuin was made abbot of Tours when the office fell vacant in the year 796, and the monastery now became an important center of educational work as a school for the training of young monks. Charlemagne seems to have felt that it would be well to release Alcuin from his duties at the palace school in order that he might devote himself without distraction to the special task of educating religious leaders. His place at the court was taken by another learned man, Theodulf, who gave attention to the problems of general education, in which Charlemagne's interest never flagged.

The significance of Charlemagne for the history of Christianity is a subject that has often invited speculation. That it was extensive in his day, and lingered in western Europe for many centuries, no one can doubt. His alliance with the papacy brought neither wealth nor new territorial possessions to the Frankish king, and it must have been prompted mainly by pious sentiment and personal ambition. Even when he accepted the imperial title, and thus perpetuated in Europe the political pattern of the Roman Empire, he had no intention of making the church in his kingdom obedient to the see of Peter in Italy. As emperor, crowned by the pope, Charlemagne required his subjects to take a new oath of allegiance to him. Although he delegated to the clergy the duty of administering this oath, he did not demand any new declaration of allegiance to the pope. Also the reforms that Boniface had instituted, for the purpose of bringing Frankish Christendom more strictly in line with Roman regulations, were zealously continued by Charlemagne. But these measures were supported for the good of the Frankish churches rather than with a view to making them conscious of any theory of papal authority. Charlemagne did not look beyond the Alps to the Roman pontiff as a lord to whom the king was a vassal—Charlemagne was no "ultramontane."

In all his dealings with the church Charlemagne acted on the assumption that he was the head of Christendom in western Europe. He summoned councils on his own initiative, and occasionally had decisions passed contrary to the papal instructions. He took under his direct control the appointment of bishops and the establishment of archbishoprics to suit the needs of his political administration. Clerical appointments were, in the last resort, subject to his will. With the monasteries also he dealt directly, often allowing them a degree of autonomy that was not at all pleasing either to the popes or the bishops. Even the condition of the local church received Charlemagne's personal supervision. He held himself competent to regulate the conduct of its members, to restrict pagan customs, to correct the defective morals of the clergy and to provide for their education. He also concerned himself very immediately with the conversion to Christianity of pagans in conquered territory, even believing it proper to order them to be baptized at the point of the sword!

Notwithstanding his freedom from papal domination, Charlemagne must be held chiefly responsible for transplanting upon European soil the imperialistic type of religious psychology that constituted a formidable barrier to the progress of an independent church among the new peoples, and gave prestige to imperially minded popes in their struggle to control the kings in the new nations. Charlemagne inculcated the ideal of inseparable union between church and state. The kingdom of God was a mighty empire governed by a single ruler in whose hand God had placed the scepter. This way of thinking was capable of being used, alike by a strong emperor or by a strong pope, to suppress the growth of a national church and to smother any awakening of democratic tendencies. While Charlemagne's favorite book was Augustine's *City of God*, it was the earthly rather than the heavenly city that caught the imagination of a ruler who was both king of the Franks and founder of the "Holy Roman Empire."

SELECTED BIBLIOGRAPHY

The appended list of books will enable readers who so desire to pursue still further the study of Christianity's expansion during the first eight centuries. A moderately extensive selection of books on the whole subject will be found in S. J. Case and others, *A Bibliographical Guide to the History of Christianity.* (Chicago, 1931.)

ENCYCLOPEDIAS

The following encyclopedias contain detailed biographical information:

Herbermann, C. G., and others, *The Catholic Encyclopedia.* 17 vols. (New York, 1907-22.)

Jackson, S. M., and others, *The New Schaff-Herzog Encyclopedia of Religious Knowledge.* (New York, 1908-12.)

Smith, W., and Wace, H., *Dictionary of Christian Biography, Literature, Sects and Doctrines.* 4 vols. (London, 1877-87.)

MAPS

Maps, that are often helpful for the student, can be found at the end of the following volumes:

Harnack, A., *Mission and Expansion of Christianity in the First Three Centuries.* 2 vols. 2d edition. (London, 1908.)

The Cambridge Medieval History, Vols. I and II. (New York, 1911 and 1913.)

See also E. McClure, *Historical Church Atlas* (London, 1897); K. Heussi and H. Mulert, *Atlas zur Kirchengeschichte* (Tübingen, 1905); W. R. Shepherd, *Historical Atlas*, 3d edition (New York, 1923), pp. 35-55.

GENERAL BIOGRAPHICAL WORKS

General works with a biographical emphasis are:

Farrar, F. W., *Lives of the Fathers.* 2 vols. Cheap reissue. (London, 1907.) First published in 1889, but still valuable; ends with Chrysostom.

Leigh-Bennett, E., *Handbook of the Early Christian Fathers*. (London, 1920.) Clement of Rome to Augustine.

McGiffert, A. C., *History of Christian Thought*. 2 vols. (New York, 1932-33.) A standard work on the theological beliefs of Christian leaders, with brief references to biographical data.

Moody, C. N., *The Mind of the Early Converts*. (London, 1920.) Ends with Origen; stresses theological opinions.

Willey, J. H., *Early Church Portraits*. (Edinburgh, 1927.) Includes Polycarp, Tertullian, Origen, Athanasius, Chrysostom, Augustine, Gregory the Great, Charlemagne; sketchy but valuable for the general reader.

The series of small volumes called "The Fathers for English Readers," published in London by the Society for Promoting Christian Knowledge, although most of the books appeared some forty odd years ago, is still useful. It includes, among others, *Ambrose*, by Archdeacon Thornton; *Athanasius* by R. W. Bush; *Augustine* by E. L. Cutts; *Basil* by R. T. Smith; *Boniface* by I. G. Smith; *Gregory the Great* by J. Barmby; *Hilary of Poitiers and Martin of Tours* by J. G. Cazenove; *Jerome* by E. L. Cutts; *Leo the Great* by C. Gore; *Patrick* by E. J. Newell; *The Venerable Bede* by G. F. Browne.

The popular series in French, "Les Saints" (Paris: Lecoffre), written by able Roman Catholic scholars, many volumes of which have passed through numerous editions, should be noted. Some of these volumes have appeared in English translations that in some cases are now out of print. They are published in London by Burns Oates and Washbourne.

ORIGINAL SOURCES

The most extensive collection in English translation of ancient Christian writings is *The Ante-Nicene Fathers* (9 vols.), *The Nicene and Post-Nicene Fathers*, First Series (14 vols.) and Second Series (14 vols.), published by Scribner's in New York. These volumes do not contain the complete works of the Greek and Latin Christian authors, and some of the translations are made from imperfect originals. There is at present in process of publication by the Society for Promoting Christian Knowledge in London (represented in the United States by the Macmillan Company of New York), a new series of "Translations of Christian Literature," several volumes of which have already appeared.

Selections from the sources have been issued in convenient form, e.g.,

Ayer, J. C., *A Source Book for Ancient Church History.* (New York, 1913.) To 787 A.D.

Kidd, B. J., *Documents Illustrative of the History of the Church.* 2 vols. (London, 1920-23.) To 461 A.D.

Wright, F. A., *Fathers of the Church: Selections from the Writings of the Latin Fathers.* (New York, 1929.) Tertullian, Cyprian, Arnobius, Lactantius, Ambrose, Jerome, Augustine.

A handy introduction to the writings of the ancient Christians is O. Bardenhewer, *Patrology: The Lives and Works of the Fathers of the Church.* Translated from the German by T. J. Shahan. (St. Louis, Mo., 1908.)

CHAPTER I

Jesus

Case, S. J., *Jesus: A New Biography.* (Chicago, 1927.)

Easton, B. S., *Christ in the Gospels.* (New York, 1930.)

Klausner, J., *Jesus of Nazareth.* (New York, 1925.)

Scott, E. F., *The Ethical Teaching of Jesus.* (New York, 1924.)

Peter

Chase, F. H., *Peter in Christian Tradition.* (Edinburgh, 1900.)

Foakes-Jackson, F. J., *Peter, Prince of the Apostles.* (New York, 1927.)

Lietzmann, H., *Petrus und Paulus in Rom.* 2d edition. (Berlin, 1927.) The most adequate discussion of the question of Peter's residence in Rome.

CHAPTER II

Paul

Enslin, M. S., *The Ethics of Paul.* (New York, 1930.)

Gardner, P., *The Religious Experience of Paul.* (New York, 1911.)

McNeile, A. H., *St. Paul: His Life, Letters and Christian Doctrine.* (Cambridge, 1920.)

Morgan, W., *The Religion and Theology of Paul.* (New York, 1917.)

The Evangelists

Cadbury, H. J., *The Making of Luke-Acts*. (New York, 1927.)
Easton, B. S., *The Gospel before the Gospels*. (New York, 1928.)
Grant, F. C., *The Growth of the Gospels*. (New York, 1933.)

CHAPTER III

Ignatius

Lake, K., *The Apostolic Fathers, with an English Translation*. (London, 1912.)

Gnostics

Burkitt, F. C., *Church and Gnosis: A Study of Christian Thought and Speculation in the Second Century*. (Cambridge, 1932.)
de Faye, E., *Gnostiques et gnosticisme*. 2d edition. (Paris, 1925.) Probably the best critical study of the subject.
Foakes-Jackson, F. J., *Christian Difficulties in the Second and Twentieth Centuries: A Study of Marcion and His Relation to Modern Thought*. (Cambridge, 1903.)
Harnack, A., *Marcion: Das Evangelium vom fremden Gott*. 2d edition. (Leipzig, 1924.) The authoritative work on Marcion.
Mead, G. R. S., *Fragments of a Faith Forgotten*. (London, 1900.) English translation of Gnostic fragments.

Justin

Carrington, P., *Christian Apologetics of the Second Century*. (London, 1921.)
Williams, A. Lukyn, *Justin Martyr: The Dialogue with Trypho*. (London, 1930.) Translation, introduction and notes.

Irenæus

Bindley, T. H., *The Epistle of the Gallican Churches*. (London, 1900.) English rendering of the document from Eusebius.
Hitchcock, F. R. Montgomery, *Irenæus of Lugdunum*. (Cambridge, 1914.)
——, *The Treatise of Irenæus of Lugdunum Against the Heresies*. 2 vols. (London, 1916.) Translation of selections with notes.
Robinson, J. Armitage, *St. Irenæus: The Demonstration of the Apostolic Preaching*. (London, 1920.) Translation with introduction and notes.

CHAPTER IV

Tertullian

Mayor, J. E. B., *Tertulliani apologeticus.* (London, 1917.) English translation of the *Apology* with introduction and notes.

Souter, A., *Tertullian concerning the Resurrection of the Flesh.* (London, 1922.)

Cyprian

Benson, C. W., *Cyprian, His Life, Times, Work.* (London, 1897.)

Blakeney, E. H., *Cyprian: De unitate ecclesiæ.* (London, 1928.) Latin text with English translation and notes.

Lacey, T. A., *Select Epistles of St. Cyprian Treating of the Episcopate.* (London, no date.) Introduction and English rendering.

Clement of Alexandria

Patrick, J., *Clement of Alexandria.* (Edinburgh, 1914.)

Tollinton, R. B., *Alexandrine Teaching on the Universe.* (London, 1932.)

——, *Clement of Alexandria: A Study in Christian Liberalism.* 2 vols. (London, 1914.)

Origen

de Faye, E., *Origen and His Work.* (New York, 1929.) A series of popular lectures, translated from the French.

——, *Origène, sa vie, son œuvre, sa pensée.* 3 vols. (Paris, 1923–28.) The most detailed critical study.

Metcalfe, W., *Gregory Thaumaturgus, Address to Origen.* (London, 1920.) Introduction and English rendering.

Patrick, J., *The Apology of Origen in Reply to Celsus.* (Edinburgh, 1892.)

Tollinton, R. B., *Selections from the Commentaries and Homilies of Origen.* (London, 1929.) English rendering.

Lactantius

Pichon, R., *Lactance: Étude sur le mouvement philosophique et religieux sous le règne de Constantin.* (Paris, 1901.) The only good critical biography available.

Chapter V

Constantine

Baker, G. P., *Constantine the Great and the Christian Revolution.* (New York, 1930.) Mainly concerned with political events.

Baynes, N. H., *Constantine the Great and the Christian Church.* (London, 1930.) A single lecture extensively annotated; a very important study.

Firth, C. H., *Constantine the Great.* (New York, 1905.)

Maurice, J., *Constantin le Grand: L'Origine de la civilization chrétienne.* (Paris, 1924.) A striking treatment; perhaps may be called "brilliant."

Athanasius

Bell, H. I., *Jews and Christians in Egypt* (London, 1924), pp. 38-120.

Burn, A. E., *The Council of Nicæa: A Memorial for Its Sixteenth Century.* (London, 1925.)

Gwatkin, H. M., *Studies of Arianism.* 2d edition. (Cambridge, 1900.)

Basil

Clarke, W. K. L., *St. Basil the Great: A Study in Monasticism.* (Cambridge, 1913.)

——, *The Ascetic Works of Saint Basil.* (London, 1925.) Introduction, translation and notes.

Deferrari, R. J., *Saint Basil. The Letters.* 3 vols. (London, 1926-29.) Greek text with English rendering, in the "Loeb Classical Library." A final volume still to be issued.

Gregory of Nyssa, *The Life of St. Macrina.* Translated by W. K. L. Clarke. (London, 1916.)

Jacks, L. V., *St. Basil and Greek Literature.* (Washington, D. C., 1922.)

Morison, E. F., *St. Basil and His Rule.* (London, 1912.)

Murphy, Margaret G., *St. Basil and Monasticism.* (Washington, D. C., 1930.)

Ambrose

de Labriolle, P., *The Life and Times of St. Ambrose.* (St. Louis, Mo., 1928.) Translated from the French.

von Campenhausen, Hans, *Ambrosius von Mailand als Kirchen-politiker.* (Berlin, 1929.) The most important recent critical work.

CHAPTER VI

John Chrysostom

Baur, C., *Der heilige Johannes Chrysostomus und seine Zeit.* 2 vols. (München, 1929-30). The most important recent biographical study.

Moore, H., *The Dialogue of Palladius concerning the Life of Chrysostom.* (London, 1921.) Introduction and English rendering.

Jerome

Cavallera, F., *St. Jérôme: sa vie et son œuvre.* Pt. I in 2 vols. (Paris, 1922.) The authoritative biography; still to be completed.

Wright, F. A., *Select Letters of St. Jerome.* (London, 1933.) Latin text and English translation; in the "Loeb Classical Library."

Augustine

D'Arcy, M. C., and others, *A Monument to St. Augustine.* (New York, 1930.)

Gilson, E., *Introduction a l'étude de Saint Augustin.* (Paris, 1931.) A very convenient and reliable introduction, with an extensive bibliography covering the vast literature of the subject.

Lesaar, H. H., *Saint Augustine.* (London, 1931.) Translated from German.

McDougall, Eleanor, *St. Augustine: A Study in His Personal Religion.* (New York, 1931.)

Montgomery, W., *St. Augustine: Aspects of His Life and Thought.* (London, 1914.)

Simpson, W. J. Sparrow, *St. Augustine's Conversion: An Outline of His Development to the Time of His Ordination.* (London, 1930.)

CHAPTER VII

Leo the Great

Gregorovius, F., *The History of the City of Rome in the Middle Ages.* (London, 1894.) Translated from the German by Annie Hamilton. Vol. I, pp. 189-230.

Regnier, A., *St. Léon le Grand.* 2d edition. (Paris, 1910.)

Benedict of Nursia

Butler, Cuthbert, *Benedictine Monachism: Studies in Benedictine Life and Rule.* (London, 1919.)

Clarke, W. K. L., *The Rule of St. Benedict.* (London, 1931.) English translation.

Gregory the Great

Batiffol, P., *St. Gregory the Great.* (London, 1928.) Translated from the French.

Dudden, F. H., *Gregory the Great: His Place in History and in Thought.* 2 vols. (London, 1905.)

Howorth, H. H., *St. Augustine of Canterbury: The Birth of the English Church.* (London, 1913.)

———, *St. Gregory the Great.* (London, 1912.)

Hutton, W. H., "Gregory the Great," in *Cambridge Medieval History*, Vol. II (New York, 1913), pp. 236-62.

Chapter VIII

Gregory of Tours

Dalton, O. M., *History of the Franks by Gregory of Tours.* 2 vols. (Oxford, 1927.) Vol. I is an elaborate introduction and Vol. II is an English translation.

Dill, S., *Roman Society in Gaul in the Merovingian Age* (New York, 1926), pp. 308-51.

Boniface

Browne, G. W., *Boniface of Crediton and His Companions.* (London, 1910.)

Kylie, E., *The English Correspondence of St. Boniface.* (London, 1924.) This is No. 19 in "The Medieval Library."

Robinson, G. W., *The Life of St. Boniface by Willibald.* Translated into English. (Cambridge, 1916.)

Williamson, J. M., *Life and Times of St. Boniface.* (London, 1904.)

Charlemagne

Davis, H. W. C., *Charlemagne.* (New York, 1900.)

Gaskoin, C. J. B., *Alcuin, His Life and Work.* (London, 1904.)

Hodgkin, T., *Charles the Great.* (New York, 1897.)

Mullinger, J. B., *The Schools of Charles the Great*. (New York, 1904.)

Turner, S. E., *Einhard, Life of Charlemagne*. (New York, 1880.) English Translation.

Wells, C. L., *The Age of Charlemagne*. (New York, 1898.)

West, A. F., *Alcuin and the Rise of the Christian Schools*. 2d edition. (New York, 1912.)

INDEX